Rocking Chair Parables

Lessons I Learned Along the Way

Patricia Seigle

Copyright © 2009 Patricia Seigle

ISBN: 978-1-60383-249-6
Published by:
Holy Fire Publishing
717 Old Trolley Road
Attn: Suite 116, Publishing Unit #116
Summerville, SC 29485

www.ChristianPublish.com

Cover Designer: Jay Cookingham

Printed in the United States of America and the United Kingdom

TO MY READERS

I have now lived well past the "*three score and ten*" we humans call a lifetime, and I find I am spending more and more time recalling events in my life. As I sit in my rocking chair, pondering the experiences I've had, so many memories come rushing back. Memories of mistakes I made, blessings I've had, joys and the sorrows, and I ask myself, why did these events occur? My little stories, based on my true experiences, are not really any different than what any number of people may have had.

As a girl in high school, I was assigned to write an essay titled, *What I want to do when I finish school.* My dream was to be a writer, a journalist, an author. I turned that assignment in to the teacher. The following day as she read my paper aloud in the class, she made a big joke of the idea of a ninth grader in Howell, Michigan, ever being a writer. So much for the idealistic ideas of a fifteen-year-old girl!

I've been making notes and scribbling little stories for several years with no plan or purpose. At least I didn't know there was a plan or a purpose. Now, I have discovered the Lord does have a plan or a purpose for these musings of mine. It was while preparing for a Bible study on the book of Jonah that the whole concept hit me.

In *The Message*, a contemporary translation of the Bible, there is an introduction to that book, which says, "Stories are the most prominent biblical way of helping us see ourselves in the 'God Story,' which always gets around to the story of God making and saving us."

It goes on to say, that stories, if they're good, can tease the reader into becoming a part of the story, to become involved in the story.

Other sources said that Jonah was considered by many not to have written the book, but was considered the narrator, or the storyteller. And didn't he have a story to tell!

In the Bible Jesus too was a story teller, as He often spoke in parables, simple little stories to which people could relate, in order to get a simple message across to them.

That word *storyteller*, connected with my spirit; I consider myself to be a storyteller. In a book which I wrote for my children and their children, I told them about the old Native American tradition of the storyteller.

She was usually the oldest woman in the tribe, and it was her duty to gather the children and the young people, and recite to them, over and over, the history of their people. I feel it is important for the people of the future to know and understand the people of their past.

Recently, I was privileged to attend a meeting in Port St. Lucie, Florida, where a man of God made the following statement, "God will not give you a dream without giving you the ability and the talent to realize that dream."

My heart leapt with joy at the confirmation of my long desired dream. Could this really be? Could this be the time?

As I sit in my rocking chair, relaxing and thanking God for all He has done for me, I feel I must share these stories with whoever needs to read them.

Whatever the result of this effort may be, I intend to plunge ahead and endeavor to have my words put into book form as directed by the Lord. What I am writing is being done in a spirit of love, intending only to bring glory to the Lord, who gave His only Son for me that I may be saved and be with Him in eternity.

If readers can look at this little book of snippets of my life as a tempting appetizer, my comment to them is, "Bon Appetite." Read, enjoy, and praise God for all of His blessings.

Jean —
I pray my memories will be a blessing to you — perhaps some of them will be familiar to you, too.
Blessings,
Pat Siegle

DEDICATIONS AND ACKNOWLEDGEMENTS

I must express my deepest gratitude and love to my family and friends, without whom this work would not have been possible. This book is for all of you.

If God had not blessed me with these people, I could not have learned the lessons I needed to learn. I realized I made many mistakes in raising my family.

A wise old woman once gave me a great bit of advice. "Do the best you can with what you have to work with."

Too often, the "things" I had to work with – good judgment, self-discipline, and common sense – left much to be desired.

I was not always right, but thank God I know I am forgiven of those things I have done which have caused hurt or anguish to those who are so precious to me. I can only trust that God will help those people I have injured realize that those mistakes were not intentional.

I must also acknowledge the efforts of those who have assisted me with the technicalities necessary for such a project. You all know who you are, and I will never forget all you have done to assist me in this project.

I cannot omit Jeanne M. Leach, my professional editor, who took a very raw manuscript and used her expertise to make it into marketable material. The Lord worked in mysterious ways when He brought her into my life, and I must remember to thank Him for that blessing as well.

FORWARD

I quote a portion of Psalm 78, from The Message.

> "Listen, dear friends, to God's truth,
> and bend your ears to what I tell you.
> I'm chewing on a morsel of a proverb;
> I'll let you in on the sweet old truths,
> stories we heard from our fathers,
> counsel we learned at mother's knee.
> We're not keeping this to ourselves;
> we're passing it along to the next
> generation--God's fame and fortune, the
> marvelous things He has done.
> So the next generation would know, and
> all the generations to come-
> Know the truth and tell the stories so
> their children can trust God. Never
> forget the works of God, but keep His
> commandments to the letter."

These words were written several hundred years before the coming of the Messiah, when the children still lived under the Law.

Praise God, we no longer must live under the law. We live in the age of grace and mercy, thanks to the shed blood of Jesus, our Savior and our Intercessor. We live in grace and mercy, but we know that this same God of love and mercy is also a God of justice.

Even though we live in grace, we still must remember the works of God and the mysterious ways He moves in our lives, if we allow Him. God loves us;

He will always love us, but we must honor His Son and claim His sacrifice for ourselves.

It doesn't matter to Him if you've always gone to church, or if your parents were Bible-believing Christians. This is a choice which we each must make for ourselves. No one can do it for you. I heard an old preacher use the expression, "Just because the cat has kittens in the oven, it doesn't make them biscuits."

The Word says, "All have sinned and come short of the glory of God." (Romans 3:23). "If we say we have no sin, we deceive ourselves, and the truth is not in us." (I John 1:8). "The just shall live by faith." (Romans 1:17). That faith must be based soundly on the fact that Jesus paid the price for our forgiveness. Even if we were the only person who ever sinned, He would have made that sacrifice. Read Galatians 3:20. "I live by faith in the Son of God, who loved me, and gave Himself for me!"

This is a choice, which we each must make for ourselves. No one can do it for you.

I made that choice in 1976 and have never once regretted it. I believe these Words so strongly that I have entrusted my entire eternity to them.

If I am wrong – a foolish, old woman – what have I lost? If I am right, what have I gained? Eternity with the Lord and all of His saints!

I don't know how many years God has planned for me; only He does. If I am still around long enough to reach the four-score mark, I will continue living to serve Him, and I pray that everything I do will bring only glory to His name.

Above all, please remember that God loves you, and this old storyteller loves you even if we have never met; I have loved you. I pray that as you ponder my little stories you can examine your own life and you will be able to see where God has been trying to teach you, to lead you, and do wonderful things through you.

May God richly bless you.

Cancer fighters

Bo K Choy
½ cp Tomato Sauce
Flounder
Strawberries
1 cup daily
Artichoke

Cal
B12, 1,000

Mag 400
D 400

TABLE OF CONTENTS

BIG SISTERS AND COAL BINS 17
SUNDAY DINNER AT GRANDMA AND
    GRANDPA'S.. 19
MY AUNT'S TOUGH LOVE 21
FIRST DAY OF SCHOOL 25
SKIPPING SCHOOL 27
HER FIRST PROM 31
THE MYSTERY OF THE MORNING GLORIES 33
LITTLE BOAT, BIG POND...................................... 37
DREAMS REALIZED.. 39
A CAT'S CHOICE 43
SWIMMING IN DEEP WATER 45
COMPANY IS COMING 47
CRUSIN' AND MUSIN'.. 49
THIS OLD HOUSE 53
LIFE ON THE RIVER... 55
MY DOG, ROSCOE 57
MEMORIES OF CCOMBAT 61
FIRST IMPRESSIONS... 63
THE STORY OF THE WEEPING WILLOW
    TREE 67
HIDE AND GO SEEK 73
MUSTANGS AND COW PONDS 79
FRIENDLY FIRE.. 81
LOOKING UP AT THE DOCK 85
BIG FAMILY, ONE BATHROOM 89
TRADING STAMPS 91
BOYS AND THEIR TOYS.. 93
IS THAT YOU, PEDRO?... 97
OUR TOWN CHARACTER 101
WHO NEEDS KIDS? 105
A CHURCH CAMP FAMILY VACATION............. 109

A RED TRACTOR 115
NEW EYEGLASSES 119
LEARNING TO DRIVE 123
GRANDMOTHER, MEET PATSY... 127
LOOK FOR ME..131
ARE THEY GOLDEN OR RUSTY? 135
AVERAGE? ABOVE? 137
TO PROTECT AND SERVE 141
PERSPECTIVES 145
THE QUICKENING..149
CORNFIELD GAMES...151
A FAREWELL REMEMBERED 153
TIME—WHAT IS IT? 159
MOTHER'S FURNITURE-MOVING FRIEND...163
CHILDREN'S CHILDREN..165
THE OTHER ROOM..169
HAIL TO THE VICTORS 171
SEED BAG DRESSES...177
WILL YOU TAKE A CHECK? 181
FAITH IN OUR PARENTS 185
DO YOU LISTEN TO YOUR WIFE?.....................189
I BEG YOUR PARDON...193
LOOK BEFORE YOU GRAB....................................195
LESSONS FROM THE SHRUBBERY 197
THE BROKEN DOLL BABY 199
CONSIDER THE TURTLE..201
ALL THINGS RELATIVE 207
THE OFFICE ASSISTANT..211
REMEMBERING THE WAITING 213
HEALING OLD WOUNDS 215
ANCHORS AND RUDDERS....................................223
ARCHIE AND LIZZIE CHAMBERLAIN 227
ARE YOU LISTENING?..233
SOMETHING'S OUT THERE! 237

SILLY BIRDS! WHY ARE YOU WALKING?.......239
TRUSTING GOD, IN SPITE OF IT ALL..............241
WEARING MASKS 243
YOU CAN FOOL SOME OF THE PEOPLE 247
A LITTLE CHILD SHALL LEAD THEM 251
UNCLE BILL'S WEDDING...............................253
BAD HABITS AND BREAKING TIMES..............257
I LOVE YOU BECAUSE..................................261
HOW MANY FOR LUNCH?..............................263
FLOATING IN AIR AND REMEMBERING.......267
ON BEING WEIGHTED DOWN 273
BURNING DAYLIGHT 275
WHAT IS BETTER THAN TWO...........................279
EXPLORING SPIRITUAL THINGS......................283
KIT AND MABEL 287
MY FIRST PERMANENT..................................289
DANCING WITH DANNY 293
VAPOR TRAILS 299
THE LAST LOVE LETTER 301
KEEP HOLD OF GOD'S HAND...........................303
PSALM 17:15...309

BIG SISTERS AND COAL BINS

Big sisters are really nice to have—most of the time. They are handy for things like helping you learn to tie shoelaces and how to sip through a straw without crimping the end. But there are the other times too.

My big sister loved to say in a singsong voice, "You're going to get in trouble!" And I usually did.

Like the time when I was about four years old and we lived across the street from the school. Attached to the rear of the building was a furnace room and a coal storage area.

One hot summer day, she and I went to the playground there to play on the swings and the slide, but instead I crawled up onto the roof of the coal area. She did the big sister routine.

"You come down from there right now!" she demanded.

As I pranced around the roof, I inadvertently did exactly what she told me to, except I fell through the opening of the coal chute. I screamed for help as I slid down the huge pile of coal, tears running down my face, which by now was covered in coal dust. My pretty little yellow sun suit was black.

Again, my sister came to my rescue by running home to get help. I kept screaming and soon my daddy's face appeared in the opening—my hero! I tried to reach his arms, but with every attempt I made to climb up the pile, I slid down more as the coal moved beneath me. I just knew I was never going to get out of there alive.

Then my six-foot-two-inch tall daddy jumped through the opening. He was still wearing the white shirt and suit pants he'd worn to church that morning, but he was right beside me as dirty as I was. He picked me up in his arms and calmed my fears, assuring me that we would both get out just fine. He held me up in his arms to my mother, who was there to take me from him. He then easily hopped out, replaced the cover securely and the four of us, coal dust and all, walked home together. After we all washed up, we had ice cream, and that tragic day ended happily.

Every time I remember the incident, I think, isn't that just like Jesus? When we are in our coal bin of sin, covered with soot, screaming for someone to help, He loves us enough to get right down in there with us, to lift us up to safety.

SUNDAY DINNER AT GRANDMA AND GRANDPA'S

When I was about four years old, my dad's family would often gather at my grandparent's home for Sunday dinner. When everyone was there, there were eleven O'Brien's, plus three spouses and four grandchildren, of whom I was the youngest.

Those dinners always provided a time of laughter and silliness, from the moment the first group arrived until the last one headed for home. I think what I liked best about going there for dinner was that everyone sat at the table. They didn't need a separate table for the children.

I remember Daddy and one or two uncles pulling the table apart to put in the extra leaves, then carefully lining up the dowels and pushing the whole thing back together. While they worked on that project, other uncles gathered chairs from other rooms in the house, plus the piano bench. My sister and I always sat on the bench. For a long time, I also had to sit on the Sears catalog on the bench in order to see over the top of the table.

When those tasks were done, the aunts would get our grandma's biggest, white tablecloth. With great flair, they would unfurl it over the table and smooth out any fold lines with their hands. They made a grand celebration of setting the table with the "good dishes" and put the silverware at each place in a precise pattern. All the while, conversation and laughter filled the house.

It's odd that I don't remember anything special that we ate. I remember Grandma hustling everyone to his or her place and Grandpa asking the blessing on the meal. Then the business of passing around all the dishes full of food began. After the main dishes were passed around, the pickles and extra goodies came next. It seemed to take a long time. Surely, the food must have gotten cold by the time that was all done. All I remember is how good everything tasted.

To finish the meal, the ladies cleared off the dirty dishes and the leftover food, if there was any. One aunt would get the little silver tray and brush to clear away any crumbs. Grandma would then enter the dining room in grand fashion, carrying a cake or whatever dessert she had made. Right behind her would be another one of the aunts carrying clean desert plates and fresh forks or spoons.

Those joyous memories are wonderful, and I treasure them. Now I'm looking forward to that supper we are promised in heaven. I've heard it called the *Marriage Supper of the Lamb*. We will all be dressed like Grandma's tablecloth, in pure white and without spot or wrinkle. What a beautiful promise is awaiting us if we believe and accept what the Bible tells us is in store for us.

MY AUNT'S TOUGH LOVE

In the winter when I turned five, I was very sick with double pneumonia. I remember the doctor coming to the house and telling my folks they had to get me to the hospital right away. I was scared and crying. Daddy wrapped me in blankets and carried me to the car, crying along with me as Mother drove us to the hospital.

That day was January 28, 1937, my birthday. I was in the hospital until May 31, over four months.

After the hospital stay, needless to say I was very weak, and the family was ready to jump to serve my every whim as if I were a princess. I soon became a spoiled brat. My Aunt Florence came to visit and was shocked to see how weak I was. She immediately told my mother that the only way for me to get my strength back would be make me do things for myself.

They all said, "Oh, she's too weak," and "I couldn't do that to her," and other similar comments.

"Well, I can and I will," Aunt Florence replied. "Get that child ready right now; she's coming home with me."

So once again, Mom bundled me up. This time the trip took me to Flint, Michigan. Aunt Florence set up a bed for me in front of the big window so I could watch the neighborhood children playing. One day, I asked her for a drink of water. She said she was too busy, and I would either have to wait until she was done, or do it myself.

I threw a spoiled brat hissy-fit and announced that I would just do it on my own.

She had been getting me out of bed, walking me from one chair to another, and then back to bed. I hadn't noticed that she had placed chairs every few feet from the bed to the sink. I managed to get about halfway to the sink, going from chair to chair, until I leaned dramatically on the nearest chair and cried, "Oh please, Aunt Florence, can't you help me?"

She turned her back to me and said again that she had chores to do, and if I wanted a drink I had to get it myself.

My nasty temper kicked in, and I made myself crawl to the next chair, stop and rest, and then go on until I reached the sink and collapsed in the chair next to it, crying. As I did that, she turned around and handed me a glass of water. That's when I noticed that she'd been crying too.

My trips from chair to chair grew longer, until one day I was allowed to walk out to the front porch. The children had been playing in the fields, and my cousin Gwen came to the house with a crown she had made of blue cornflowers.

She put it on my head and said, "Now, you a really are a princess."

For those few weeks of her tough love, I really thought I hated my Aunt Florence. As I grew older, I realized that she was right. The only way I would ever get strong again was to use the muscles, which had been suffering from atrophy. Her careful planning of where to place each chair allowed me to progress slowly. It took weeks of baby steps before I was ready to go play with the other children.

Our Father God, on occasion has to use tough love on us too. He often has to allow us to suffer through something we think is dreadful, but in reality, it is something He has planned for our good. He is with us as we take baby steps. I'm sure tears roll down his cheeks as He watches us struggle, just as they did for my Aunt Florence.

There have been many times in my life that I doubted His love for me, and felt that if He really loved me, He would make things easier for me.

But one lesson I have learned is that we don't build up our strength during the easy times. We only get stronger in our faith after we take baby steps through the struggles and build our faith up to the point when we take bold strides.

FIRST DAY OF SCHOOL

I started kindergarten when I was still four years old. The rule stated that a child had to be five by December 31st to begin school. I never figured out how I started at four when my birthday wasn't till the end of January. That meant I was the youngest kid in the class.

I was proud that day. My big sister and her friends allowed me to follow behind them as we walked the six or seven short blacks to school. I felt so grown up; I was with the *big* girls.

My pride was riding for a fall. You see, I didn't know kindergarteners only went to school a half a day, and the big kids went until after three in the afternoon. That meant I would have to walk home by myself.

Homeward bound, I remember strolling along, feeling so grand and very cocky, when I suddenly realized that I didn't know where I was. I remember walking and crying, and to this day, I'm not sure how I got home. We lived in a small town, so probably some kind soul knew who I was took me home, but I don't remember.

The next day, I was too terrified to go to school again, but once again my big sister came to my rescue. She held my hand and made me count how many streets we had to cross before we came to the corner of the street that went directly to the school. Then she made me look at all four houses on the corners and find something about each one to remember so I would know where to turn.

That afternoon, when she came home from school, I ran to meet her, proud that I had been able to find my way home all by myself.

"I turned at the house with the peticia binds," I crowed. Translated, that meant the house with the *Venetian* blinds. She didn't let me live that down for years.

Have you ever been lost? Have you ever walked and cried for someone to help you find your way home? Try Jesus! He's always there waiting for you to ask Him to help.

SKIPPING SCHOOL

My son was a senior in high school, and there weren't many things he hadn't gotten into or tried. A true teen rebel, he tested his parents every day to see how far he could go.

This particular day, I received a phone call from the school, asking me to come to the principal's office as soon as I could. Instant stomach cramps from acid pouring into the digestive track hit me, along with the thought, *Good grief, what is it this time?*

I hurried as fast as I could and walked into the office, hands shaking, my entire body vibrating – a combination of anger and anticipation. I only had to walk into the room to know what the problem was; the unmistakable smell immediately assaulted my nose.

The principal explained to me that my son and his buddy had cut out of school before the lunch break, and returned about an hour or so later. They had stopped at the party store and bought a six-pack, which they consumed between them.

"Okay, what's your story?" I asked my son as I turned to him.

He solemnly swore the principal and teachers were wrong; he said he hadn't been drinking.

Taking a deep breath, I counted to ten. "You haven't been drinking? Do you think I just fell off the turnip truck?"

Again, he swore he hadn't had a drink.

I found it amazing how fast a mother's mind can work when it has to. A dozen different thoughts came in and out of my brain. What is the best way to handle this? What is with this kid? He cuts out, drinks beer, and then goes back to school?

"Okay, if you haven't been drinking, you won't mind going to the sheriff's office and have a Breathalyzer test done, would you? We'll just go there right now."

I took him by his sleeve and we went directly there. Of course, the test proved what we already knew – at least three bottles of beer.

Then he became penitent, ashamed of himself, and asked for forgiveness, swearing that he would never do it again. Well, of course I would forgive him, but he still had to face the consequences of his mistake. We took his car away for two weeks. There isn't a much harsher punishment for a teenage boy than to be without his wheels, especially when he had worked hard to earn the money to buy it.

I lay in bed that night fretting about him, concerned about what else he would find to get into, and it hit me hard. How many times have I pulled an equally stupid trick and tried to bluff my way out of it too? But my Father God isn't fooled any easier than I was, and He didn't have to take me to the sheriff to prove it.

Isn't it wonderful to know that He loves us anyway? He is always ready to love and forgive, but we have to realize that we too must face the consequences of our sin, and it us usually much more than losing a car for two weeks. Sometimes the choices we willingly make will have consequences that will affect us, as well as those we love, for the rest of our lives.

As St. Paul wrote in I Corinthians 11:28, "Let a man (or a woman) examine himself." (NKJV – parenthetical phrase added by author for emphasis.)

Our Father loves us, but He expects us to be honest with Him. He didn't just fall off of the turnip truck either.

HER FIRST PROM

It was the evening of my granddaughter's first prom, and we were anxious to see her in her new gown. This little girl had grown to the point that when I stood next to her, my shoulder would fit under her armpit. Tonight she looked like a princess. Howard and I decided to go see her, take pictures, and then stop for a bite to eat on the way home.

I knew she would be lovely, but I was not prepared for the breathtaking creature, who stood in front of me. Her strapless gown was exactly the right tint of pink to complement her skin tones. Her hair had been styled, with tiny flowers arranged in it.

When I walked into the room, her mother placed a dainty necklace with a small heart around her neck and tiny, diamond stud earrings in her ears. The sight of her overwhelmed me. For a finishing touch, they sprinkled glitter over her head and shoulders. The tiny pieces sparkled like small diamonds, reflecting the lights as they clung to her skin and hair.

I hugged her with tears in my eyes and pride that only a *gramie* can feel! When the photo session ended, we left before her young man arrived.

As we drove to our favorite restaurant, I thought about how much I loved all of my grandchildren, and how proud I was of all of them.

We were seated in our usual spot, and as our waitress approached, she asked, "Who's going to the prom?"

I was amazed that she would know, and I asked her if she was a mind reader or something.

31

"No," she replied. "You have glitter all over you. My girls wear it too."

Of course, I hadn't realized that while hugging her, the sparkly things had rubbed off onto my clothes.

I wonder... when I spend time with Jesus in prayer and worship; do His sparkles rub off onto me? Can people see a change in me? Do I reflect a bit of His glory? Is He as proud of me when we've spent time together as I was of my granddaughter?

I pray that my life will reflect His glory, and that I will never do anything to tarnish His image.

THE MYSTERY OF THE MORNING GLORIES

It was a gorgeous October day in central Kentucky. Cecil B. De Mille, one of Hollywood's most famous early directors, would have ordered this kind of day for a movie, if he could have. Although the temperature was in the sixties, the sun shining down from a cloudless, azure sky was warm and comforting on my skin. Words cannot describe the color of the leaves. As the breezes circulated through the trees, the leaves fell, and the sun glinting on them made it look as if it were raining gold.

We had come there with our camper and motorcycle. Our idea of fun was to get on a road and see where it took us. That day would be a real winner.

I rode behind my husband and enjoyed looking around. As we left our campsite and started down the two-lane, blacktop road, we rounded a curve and were surprised to see we were passing under the interstate highway. On our left was a small lake, surrounded on all sides by steep hills.

Circling the lake, we neared a campground and a picnic area. Families were enjoying what may have been their last cookout of the season. As children romped and played, some of the men threw their fishing lines into the lake, perhaps trying to catch supper, and the women rested in their chairs around the campfire. We could hear someone playing a guitar and a group sang some of the old gospel hymns. I wondered if they would have invited us to join them if we had stopped.

Passing the lake, the blacktop ended and we found ourselves on a gravel road, gradually climbing the hills. The higher we went, the narrower the road became. Now it was a "two tracker," and the trees were growing so closely together that we had to duck our heads as we passed under the lower boughs.

The Honda labored under the weight of the two of us, and the steepness of the climb was more than it could handle.

"I knew I should have bought the Harley," my husband muttered.

We stopped for a break, munching on apples and sipping from the water bottles stowed in the backpack. As we stretched our legs, he called out, "Look! There's an old split rail fence."

It was nearly smothered by the overgrown weeds and bushes. I threw one leg over it, intending to explore its hidden treasures.

"I don't think that a good idea," he warned.

"Why not?" I asked.

"There's probably poison ivy or snakes back in there."

His logic convinced me, and I gingerly pulled my leg back, settling to explore from the road. Suddenly I saw a speck of blue peeking through the weeds. The blue was Morning Glories, still in bloom. I told him to go on up the hill and wait for me; I'd walk up.

All I could think of was those Morning Glories. How did they get there? Did that old split rail fence once edge the yard of a log cabin? If I'd walked further back, what might I have found? Perhaps there would have been part of a foundation of a cabin, or maybe a stone chimney. There are many stone chimneys standing alone in that part of Kentucky.

Surely, a woman had planted them. Perhaps she had brought the start of the plant with her from her parent's home when she moved to this place with her young husband. Could it have been seventy-five or a hundred years or more when they lived here? Were they pioneers? Where did they come from?

When I reached the top of the hill, Howard was patiently waiting. As we rode on, the bower of trees began to thin out. The "two-tracker" widened, and soon we were on a graded, gravel road. As we broke out into a clearing, the gravel turned to blacktop. We made a wide curve to the east, and suddenly we were on a bridge, crossing over that same interstate highway.

The rest of the ride remained on two lanes through the little valley. We passed an old schoolhouse, called the "Redbud School." On our left was a big, old barn with a huge graveled parking lot. On our right stood an old, gray building with a sign that identified it as the "Boardin' House."

Nearly thirty years have passed since we made that visit to Rockcastle County, Kentucky, to that little place called "Renfro Valley." Sometimes on our way driving north or south on I-75, we get off at that exit and drive through, but it's all different now. The Bluegrass Country music is still played there in the old barn. Now there's also a new barn for the modern country music, which uses amplifiers and drums.

Many things, along with new and old buildings have been added, and I suppose for those folks who live there the changes are good financially. I hope so.

Still, my heart always goes back to that day, to the split rail fence and the Morning Glories.

I wonder again, who was she? How did she get there? Where did she go? As she sowed seeds, which lived long after she was gone, did she ever wonder about how long those seeds would last?

Thinking of her made me wonder; *Years after I am gone, will there be anyone or anything that will show a sign that I was here?*

The only things I can do which will last are those things that glorify God. Buildings and material will be gone, like whatever kind of a house had been in that valley.

Lord, I pray that I will be a good sower of seeds for You. Use me, I pray.

LITTLE BOAT, BIG POND

In the summer of 1964, we spent some time in a cottage at a nearby lake. A small boat and motor were included in the package. One Sunday afternoon, my husband, his friend, and I took the little boat out for a joyride.

We were heading back to the dock when several big boats with IO's, inboard/outboard engines, raced the length of the lake. As they made their turn to race back in the other direction, their multiple wakes created a major problem for us.

My back was turned, so I couldn't see what was happening.

"Move toward me—now!" our friend said sharply to me, and I did. He had seen the large waves coming toward us, threatening to swamp our little boat.

As I moved toward him, the shifting of my weight caused the bow of the boat to come up high enough that the wake didn't break fully over the bow and cause it to go down. However, enough water came in to leave us with about two inches freeboard.

The racers quickly stopped and moved slowly beside us as we headed for the shore. When we ran aground, I stepped out into waist-high water. The racers helped my husband and his friend get the boat to the dock as I walked to the shore. After that experience, I became very aware of the damage that can be caused by the wake of a boat.

We can learn a lesson from boats and their wakes. Too often in life, we race along, busy with whatever is on our mind, and we don't stop to think about the damage we may be leaving in our wake.

We may never cause someone's boat to sink, but we can leave behind hurt feelings, broken hearts, and destroyed relationships.

Marine law states that a boat owner is liable for any damage caused by his wake.

The Bible tells us to do unto others, as you'd have them do unto you.

Before you speak, before you act, look over your shoulder to see if someone may be injured by your wake.

DREAMS REALIZED

My husband was a *Depression Baby*. For those too young to remember, the depression years from 1929 through the 1930's were a time of great financial loss, joblessness, hunger, and very hard times in general. He never had toys like youngsters have today. I recall him telling me about one Christmas, when all he got was one orange.

As he grew up, Howard worked wherever he could. One year, he worked in an apple orchard, cutting the grass with a sickle for one dollar a day. He gave his earnings to his grandparents to help with the family expenses. Eventually, he did his time in the military. In time, he found and married me; and I learned his second nature was to be thrifty—to the point of being cheap—not because he wanted to be that way; it was because he *had* to be that way to survive.

Early in our marriage, I remember him standing next to a small lake, wishing he could have a small boat from which to fish. A few years passed before he was finally able to buy a fourteen foot runabout—a dream come true for him.

The first weekend we were free, he had me pack a big picnic lunch. We and another couple drove to the nearby lake which had a public boat-launching site. We waited our turn to launch. While we girls packed the goodies in the boat, the fellows moved the car and trailer to the parking lot.

We pulled away from the dock and headed toward the center of the lake, feeling as if we were among the idle rich. Things were going smoothly until the boat suddenly stopped even though the motor was running. We had run aground on a sand bar in the middle of the lake. As we struggled to push away from the sand, which held us firmly, people around were getting a big laugh out of our situation. Somehow the joy of being a boat owner didn't last too long after that experience, because Howard soon sold it.

Boats of various sizes came and went at our house. His last one was a thirty-foot cabin cruiser, which he had bought for "a deal". After a couple summers of enjoying it, he discovered that dreaded dry rot had set in. He worked two more summers to get all of the bad wood out, replacing it with new teak or cedar, and then refinishing it. I think for him the woodworking was a labor of love because once he had her seaworthy again, he sold it.

Motorcycles were another of my husband's passions through the years. His dream bike was a 1951 Harley Davidson with full dress, complete with leather saddle bags. By the time it arrived on the scene, he was in his late fifties, and some of his strength began to wane. We had some lovely rides on it though. One evening he went for a ride by himself.

Someone ran a stop sign and pulled in front of him. To avoid a collision, Howard had to lay the bike down. After he had vented his anger by stomping the gravel into the road, he tried to set it back upright and found he didn't have the strength to lift it up by himself. Fortunately, a neighbor came along and helped him put it up on its wheels, and when he got home that day he was ready to sell that too.

Have you ever dashed headlong into something and found yourself run aground in a sandbar in life?

Have you ever had a dream realized only to find that there was no satisfaction in it?

Ecclesiastes says in Chapter 2:10-11, "I was pleased with everything I did, and this pleasure was the reward for all my hard work. But then I looked at what I had done, and I thought about all my hard work. Suddenly I realized that it was useless, like chasing the wind." (NCV)

The only way to find peace of mind and true fulfillment is to find a personal relationship with Christ. Only He can give you the peace that passes all understanding.

A CAT'S CHOICE

Howard's grandparents had a small truck farm where they raised vegetables and fruit, which they sold to the *summer people*. The only accommodation they made to their age was to have rough, wooden benches scattered around under the shade trees at the end of the garden rows. Underneath those benches, they always kept a few bushel baskets to make carrying their harvest to the house easier.

There was also a raggedy-eared, old battle-scarred tomcat, whose job was to keep down the mouse population. He was a typical farm cat, making his home in one of the outbuildings or wherever he felt like sleeping each night. *Smudge* got his name from the mark on his upper lip. He was crowding sixteen years of age when the event occurred.

One day while taking a breather on one of the benches, Granddad noticed a mouse run under one of the baskets. He called the cat, who was independent and not a pet, but would come when called. Smudge had lived around people long enough to know that when the old man called him while in the garden, there was a good possibility there were mice to be caught.

He came running, stopped at the farmer's feet, and looked Granddad straight in the eye.

"Are you ready, cat?" he asked, as he lifted the basket with his cane.

This was a jackpot! Five mice were hidden there. Instantly, the fearless hunter leapt, spreading his front paws wide; he managed to catch two with each foot, and the remaining one he grabbed in his mouth.

Now the cat had a problem. Both paws and his mouth were full. What to do next? In his eagerness to make sure he had a good meal, he had "bitten off more than he could chew." Should he release the one in his mouth, or those trapped beneath his large, front paws?

His greed had put him in an unpleasant situation. Have you ever been in a similar state of affairs? Have you ever had your hands full while trying to make life more comfortable?

Jesus told us not to worry about tomorrow. He said that the birds of the air don't sow or reap, yet the Father cares for them. Aren't you more precious to the Father than they?

SWIMMING IN DEEP WATER

My husband told me a story about an experience he had during World War II in the Philippine Islands. Manila and Baguio had been retaken, and the island of Luzon was secured. His outfit was sent to a place on the Lingayan Gulf for rest and relaxation.

The officers decided this might be an ideal time for the troops to get more practice disembarking from the troop ships, which would eventually carry them to another battle, the invasion of Japan. The boys had to go over the side of the big ship and down to the Landing Craft Troops (LCT's). The LCT's were smaller vessels, which could maneuver to the shore to give easier access for the troops who had to land on enemy soil.

These vessels bobbed like corks in the ocean alongside the big troop ships. To make this transfer, the boys had to use large cargo nets for rope ladders. For this practice, they were to be dressed as they would if they were going into an invasion situation.

For Howard, this meant carrying a full field pack, which included an M-1 Carbine rifle, a belt full of clips of ammo for the rifle, helmet, first aid kit and shovel, at least four hand grenades, and a .30 caliber, air-cooled machine gun. In total, it weighed nearly as much, or more, than his one hundred and twenty pound frame.

His expression looked grim as he told how several of the boys had lost their grip and fell into the water between the ship and the LCT.

"There was nothing anyone could do to help them," he said. "They sank rapidly below the surface."

He quickly returned to the R & R part of the story. They were camped on a beautiful, sandy beach in the shade of palm trees. He said it looked like a movie set with thousands of extras and lots of noise.

One day in his free time he decided to go for a swim in the ocean. They had periods where they had worn the same, sweaty, dirty clothes for days or weeks on end. Thinking about that made the idea of the warm ocean water sound even better.

He was relaxing, enjoying the water and the air, when he suddenly realized that he was a long way from shore. As he tried to swim toward the beach, a rip tide caught him and took him farther out to sea.

He yelled repeatedly, but no one could hear him. Somehow he knew the thing to do was to swim parallel to the shore, so he did. Before long he escaped the pull of the tide. He finally was able to make it back to the beach, where he collapsed, exhausted.

Have you ever been in a similar situation? Have you ever been relaxed, enjoying yourself and not realize you were being caught up and swept away from safety? You were alone and no one could hear your cries for help?

Have you cried out to Jesus, and asked Him to save you? He's standing by, waiting for you to surrender yourself to Him.

COMPANY IS COMING!

During World War II, my mother's cousin, Lawrence, was stationed at the U.S. Army barracks at Fort Custer, Michigan, about eighty to one hundred miles from our town. When he and a buddy had been given a three-day pass, he called my mother to see if he could stay with us, since he had no place else to go. She told him to get bus tickets for him and his friend and come to Howell. They could stay with us, and she'd show them the town, what there was of it.

They hadn't seen each other since my mother visited their home in Stevens Point, Wisconsin, in 1940.

As the day neared for the two soldiers to arrive, my mother launched my sister and me into a major house cleaning frenzy. We washed windows, curtains, floors and walls, along with the entire door trim. Every shelf was emptied and scoured, and items were replaced after they too were washed.

As a ten year old, this was not my idea of fun. The kitchen cupboards were made of bead board; I think that's what they called it. There were vertical grooves staggered in rows of five, then rows of three, and back to five. Mother insisted that each groove be scrubbed with a toothbrush, and of course, she provided the proper tool.

About the time I thought I was done, I came to the two top shelves of the pantry. Those shelves were never to be touched. They held her emergency supplies for use in case she couldn't work or some other disaster occurred. I was sure she wouldn't allow me to touch them. Wrong! I had to remove every can, box, and bag, scrub the shelf beneath them, then wipe off each item,

47

being certain to replace them with the newest in the back and oldest in the front. Whew!

When I thought I had finally pleased her, she said, "Now, get some clean water and soap and scrub the bathroom floor; and be sure you get each one of the claw-feet of the bathtub, even the one in back!"

I had to crawl on my belly to do them, and I kept bumping my head on the tub bottom.

The day finally came when two, handsome soldiers arrived on the bus amid much laughter and tears. They looked so sharp in their uniforms. Lawrence's friend was a Polish boy, named Dominic Slusarski.

For some reason, Dominic and I hit it off right away. He would start to tell a joke in his heavy Polish accent and would have trouble with the punch line in English. Somehow, I knew what he was trying to say, and we'd giggle together about that.

It was a great time for our family, laughing and treasuring each minute, especially when the time came for them to catch the bus back to camp.

I don't think I'll ever forget the time with them, or the time spent in preparing for their visit.

One day Jesus will call me to say it's time for me to go home. When I appear before His throne, my soul will be cleaner than that bathroom, because the *Master Cleaner* has cleansed me.

Have you submitted your "claw feet" to Him to be scrubbed clean? He is waiting to do it for you, if you'll only ask Him.

CRUSIN' AND MUSIN'

The idea of taking a five night cruise, stopping in Limon, Costa Rica, going through the Panama Canal, touring a banana plantation, spending a day on a private island and touring Nassau, in the Bahamas, sounded like a fairy tale to me. Yet, that's exactly what I was doing.

I felt as if I should pinch myself to see if this was reality or just a dream. As I relaxed in the lounge chair on the cabin's balcony each night, I tried to comprehend it all. The moon shone bright and full. There were no clouds to obscure the stars, and I had never seen so many all at once.

As the ship slipped silently through the water, its wake created a trail of various colors, reflecting the light of the moon in the darkness. The whole effect was so overwhelming, I nearly wept in awe.

The last day of our cruise, we were in the Straits of Florida, with Florida to the north and Cuba to the south. We knew we were there, even though we could see no sign of land.

"Look, over there!" I heard someone call out.

In the vast expanse of the water, I saw a small, rubber boat—a very small rubber boat. I counted seven people perched on the sides of the craft, perhaps ten or twelve inches above water.

The Captain brought our ship to a halt and slowly came near to the side of the fragile craft. Every balcony on the starboard side of the ship quickly filled with people leaning over the rail in an effort to see what was happening.

The people on the tiny boat paddled to the side of the ship, and several decks below, a hatch opened and a crewman tossed out a line. Several more hands reached out to help the people come aboard, but they refused.

Here they were, bouncing around like a cork, somewhere in the middle of a ninety-mile-wide stretch of water, and they refused to board the large ship! The sea was incredibly calm now, but that could change in a matter of minutes.

The crewmen passed life jackets to the six men and one woman. I could hardly believe they had no floatation devices of any sort. Next, the crew passed water and food to them, and then they paddled the tiny craft away. The Captain announced they were Cubans fleeing their homeland, desperately trying to reach a free land.

Of course, the Captain had called the U.S. Coast Guard and stood by until they arrived. It wasn't long before we could see the cutter moving swiftly toward us. It was fascinating to watch the young seamen launch their craft. It looked to be a *Zodiac*, similar to the ones I'd seen on television. As small as it looked from our distance, it was twice the size of the refugee's boat.

The refugees tried to resist them, but they had no option. Maritime Law and U.S. regulations are very clear. They had to be detained, and then returned to their homeland. Who knows what their fate would be there?

Our ship began her gradual turn and headed toward our port in Florida. The weather forecast was for winds to pick up, with rain storms that evening. I couldn't help but think of those seven people. I wondered what could have been so bad that they would literally risk their lives to escape.

I am so comfortable and safe in my life, so extremely blessed; could I ever reach a point where such dire measures would even be considered?

What would my reaction be if some powerful tyrant took over my nation? What would I do if I were suddenly not free to come and go as I please? If I couldn't go to a supermarket, where shelves groan under their loads of fresh and canned goods, and a variety of dairy and frozen foods? What if I could no longer worship God in the church of my choice, or state my religious beliefs in public—if my family and I were taken as slaves to serve some sadistic taskmaster, which happens in African nations all the time?

What would I do? What would *you* do?

THIS OLD HOUSE

It was a very old, neglected house, which sat close to our property line. The owner was a less–than-desirable neighbor. When his health forced him into a nursing home, his family was eager to sell the house.

The same afternoon the realtor had them sign the papers, she came directly to our house to let us know it was available. With their asking price being so reasonable, we jumped at the opportunity to buy it. The five acres it sat on was well worth the price. If it were ours, we could control who would be our next-door neighbors. We closed on the deal the next day.

To describe the condition of the interior is difficult. Suffice to say, we gutted the house and everything in it, filling a large dumpster several times.

As my husband tore out what passed as kitchen cabinets, he discovered the sink had been drained into a five-gallon bucket, which had not been emptied in quite some time. So long, in fact, that the floor was rotten, as well as some of the floor joists.

He tore out the bad wood and put in a new foundation to support new joists. As the project moved along, we kept making discoveries of things that would need demo work before we could do new work.

As a year passed, my husband put in new electrical wiring and plumbing, new floors and new carpeting, new insulation, and new sheet rock. He rebuilt the stairway to the bedroom upstairs. We worked as a team,I did the scrubbing and painting, laid tile floors, etc. We turned that ramshackle, old place into a charming, two-bedroom home, a neat little cottage, or as I called it, a dollhouse.

New roofing, new vinyl siding, and landscaping made it an attractive neighbor. People would often stop in to say hello as we were working, and they'd comment that they just couldn't believe the old shack could be saved, much less look good.

I often think how my life was like that old house before I gave my life to Christ. When I invited Him into my heart; He came in with His spiritual cleaning supplies, His forgiveness, His Father's grace and mercy, and the power of the Holy Spirit.

He cleaned and scrubbed, tore out the rotten joists of bad habits and put in a new foundation. He's been working in me for several years, and every now and then He has to go into a dark recess to find something that smells bad and gets rid of that too.

Have you ever thought about asking Jesus to remodel and restore your life? If you invite Him in, be prepared. He will be thorough. He'll clean every closet of your heart, the attic of your mind, and even the dark corners of the basement, if you let Him.

People will be amazed that your old house can be saved and look so good too.

LIFE ON THE RIVER

For two summers, we kept my husband's thirty-foot Owens cruiser in a small marina on the Saginaw River, just south of Bay City, Michigan. The river wound a serpentine trail from its mouth at Saginaw Bay several miles, through Bay City and south into Saginaw.

Freighters often passed our dock, going to and from Saginaw. Their outbound cargo might have been soybeans, sugar beets, or iron ore up-bound to the big General Motors Gray Iron Plant. The channel was twenty to twenty-five feet deep. Just outside of the buoy markers, it tapered quickly to six-or eight-foot depths.

It was interesting to see these big ships maneuver, trying to stay in the channel as the river twisted and turned. In one spot the ships had to come almost to a full stop and pivot in order to not run aground. Occasionally, the shop's pilot would make a mistake and run into the shoals. We were so close we could hear the engines rev as he tried to back off and float free.

One July 4th weekend, a freighter was grounded so badly the captain had to call for two tugboats to get his ship free. Crowds formed on the shore, as well as in smaller boats, to watch his struggle. When the ship was free again, horns sounded and whistles blew in celebration.

On an especially dark night I couldn't sleep, so I sat on the aft deck, wrapped in a heavy sweater. I was enjoying the breeze and the night sounds, when something moving caught my eye. It was a huge spotlight moving over the surface of the water. It stopped moving as soon as it illuminated the red buoy on the starboard side of the river. While it stayed still, a second light began searching the opposite side of the river until it found the green buoy.

That was the way the ship's pilot steered her way up the river, one finger of light searching for the next marker, while the other light held steady on the nearest one. Without following the channel markers, she would have run aground. Moving carefully, finding one marker at a time, she maneuvered the winding, twisting current safely.

I learned a valuable lesson that night. If I live my life as that ship moved in the river—one step, one day, one marker at a time—trusting Jesus as my pilot, I'll avoid the shoals.

I must not try to see what is coming a mile upstream. Jesus taught in Matthew 6:34, "Therefore do not worry about tomorrow, for tomorrow will worry about its own things. Sufficient for the day is its own trouble." (NKJV)

MY DOG, ROSCOE

I found Roscoe one summer while we had our boat moored at the Narrows of Lake Charlevoix in northern Michigan. The marina owners had a small coffee shop with living quarters in the rear. When no one was around, I would often sit in their kitchen drinking coffee and chatting with the owner, Lorna.

She had a sweet, little Cocker Spaniel named Sassy, who'd had a gentleman caller earlier that year, and found herself "in a family way." No one knew for certain who the father was, just a wayfaring stranger. The five puppies she had were adorable. As they grew, Lorna allowed the puppies to frolic around in the kitchen.

One of them would always come up to me, play with my shoestrings, and generally charm me. He had short, black hair, except for tan eyebrows and toes. The shape of his head gave me the idea that his daddy might have been part Doberman, or Shepherd.

I picked him up, looked at him straight in the eye, and said, "Hello there, Roscoe." I have no idea where I found that name, but it stuck.

When the time came for the puppies to find their new homes, Roscoe came home with me. He grew to be about twenty-four inches high. We became incredibly close. He followed me everywhere I went, and when I sat in my chair, he jumped into my lap.

The following winter, we planned a dinner party for friends. I wanted to make Swiss steak, which was a favorite with many folks. I had four nice pieces of round steak to prepare. First I trimmed the fat from each piece and rendered it down in the pan. As each piece browned, I'd take it out and put it aside to deal with later.

My daughter sat in the kitchen, talking about something, when she idly picked up a piece of the cooled, crisp fat and called Roscoe to give him a treat.

Roscoe never looked at her. His eyes followed every movement of my hands. I had cut the steak into serving portions, pounded each piece, and dredged them in flour seasoned with spices. As each piece was browned, it would go into the roasting pan. Each layer of meat was covered with sliced onions, then another layer of meat and a layer of onions until there was enough for eighteen to twenty people.

By the time this was complete, the aroma in the kitchen was enough to make everyone's mouth water. All this time, Roscoe sat beside me, his head moving as his eyes followed every movement of my hands. Even while my girl was trying to coax him to her, holding out the crisp pieces to him, he only watched me.

That day, the Lord used that little black dog to teach me a lesson. A scripture came to my mind, Hebrews 11:1, "Faith is the substance of things hoped for, the evidence of things not seen." (NKJV). We do not hope for things we can see; they are already there! We hope for things which we do not see but trust we will receive them.

Faith is an inward assurance, trust, or reliance on someone or something. Roscoe had inner assurance –he trusted me.

The world will tempt us with things which really look good to us, maybe even smell wonderful – things which by themselves may not do us harm. We must not settle for "good" when Jesus has something "excellent" for us.

We must live our lives with Christ as Roscoe did with me that day. I must make myself keep focused on Jesus and claim His promises for my own.

MEMORIES OF COMBAT

My husband didn't speak very often of his times in combat in the Philippine Islands in World War II. He did on one occasion tell of a time when they were up in the mountains so high that they were in the clouds.

He said that they were moving slowly along a narrow, mountain trail, single file, under orders not to show any light or make any noises. They called it "Light and Sound Discipline."

Suddenly, the silence was broken by the bark of the Browning Automatic Rifle (B.A.R.) carried by the soldier in front of him.

Startled by the sudden noise, Howard whispered, "What did you do that for?"

"Didn't you see him?" his comrade whispered hoarsely.

Telling the story, he said, "I hadn't seen anything until I looked at the ground in front of me and saw the enemy's rifle pointed right between my legs with the safety off. The Japanese soldier had me in his sights and had literally been cut in two by the rapid fire of my buddy's gun before he could pull his trigger and kill me."

Another event he related was of a time they'd been surrounded for over thirty days on the top of a mountain. He had dug a foxhole big enough for himself, his gear, and several boxes of ammunition for the 30 caliber air-cooled machine gun he kept with him wherever he went, and they hadn't gone anywhere for quite awhile. His job was to maintain crossfire if he saw anything move on the ridge approaching their position.

He continued to say, "The noise of our artillery being fired every five minutes had beaten a tempo into my head, when suddenly there was a new and different sound. I'd heard it before, but never this close. It was Japanese mortar fire. The first explosion I heard was a few yards behind me. The second was a few yards in front of me. I knew where the third round was going to land."

"My orders were to never to leave my weapon, but I figured the army would give me a new one, and I took off like a scared rabbit. When I looked back over my shoulder, the third mortar shell had hit. My machine gun, my possessions, and even my hole were all gone!"

In our spiritual life, we often find ourselves doing combat with our enemy. I wonder if sometimes we might be smug about our position. Thank God we can have our fellow Christians, who care enough to alert us, to be there in those times to make us aware of the upcoming danger.

Perhaps our life has been going pretty smoothly and we let down our guard. We can become so used to the daily struggle, or the routine, that we become unaware of the newest snare that's been laid for us, oblivious of the danger.

If something unusual happens, are we aware enough to realize that the next thing to happen could destroy us? Do we realize that there are times when we must flee temptation and cling to our faith in God's grace to save us?

FIRST IMPRESSIONS

I knew that admitting my husband to the hospital was going to be difficult. To begin with, his age was a problem, in addition to the many side effects of diabetes. These factors made for a traumatic experience for both of us. To complicate matters even more, he was almost totally deaf, even with his best hearing aids. After being together for nearly fifty-seven years, I was about the only person able to communicate with him. As a result, I had to serve as a sort of translator between him and the medical staff.

With his disability, background noise of any type made it extremely difficult for him to sort out the sounds of words that enabled him to understand what was being said to him. Hospitals are famous for background noise. This one was no exception.

The young woman at the Admitting Desk sympathized with us, but told us that unfortunately the hospital was full. There were no private rooms available. Trusting the Lord to care for us, I struggled to follow the young man pushing the wheelchair through the halls at a slow gallop.

A young man, who was trying to sleep, occupied the bed by the door. As they maneuvered the wheelchair around him, they bumped his bed and their conversations roused him. Finally, Howard was settled in a bed, and when the nurses had finished doing all those things they had to do, the room settled down and became quiet.

That was when I first saw her; I shook my head and thought, "Her husband will be my husband's roommate? Oh boy!"

63

She had on these black, low rider jeans, with quarter-size silver studs down the outer seams. Between the jeans and the high rider tee shirt, there was a gap of three to four inches, which allowed me to see the big butterfly tattoo on her lower back, and the rings in her navel. Her hair was dark, but had been streaked blonde and was spiked on the top of her head. Huge silver hoops dangled from her ears.

As she made herself comfy by kicking off her shoes, I was impressed by the purple/brown nail polish on her toes and by the number of rings she wore on each toe. Her shoes were clogs, with platform soles about three inches high.

It was all too easy for me to make a judgment as to what kind of a young person she was.

I soon learned how wrong I was. After my husband was established in his hospital bed and the confusion had settled down, she peeked around the curtain and said, "I've got some chocolate Baskin and Robbins ice cream in the freezer, if he'd like some."

When I thanked her and told her that he didn't like chocolate, she giggled, "There really is something wrong with him, isn't there? Doesn't like chocolate? *Everybody* likes chocolate!"

Hoping to redeem the time, I took my New Testament with Psalms from my purse. I always find comfort in Psalms, but that day my brain kept focusing on the "what ifs," distracting what my spirit was trying to do. So I laid the book down and looked out the window. There wasn't much to look at except the parking garage and the doctor's parking area.

As the hours passed, her phone conversations with her family made clear the love they shared. She spoke with her son, who would be six the next day and reassured him that it might be late, but Daddy would be home today. She asked him to make a really big *Welcome Home Daddy* sign. Then, after a pause she gently said, "I know, punkin. Daddy really misses you too."

She spoke to her grandfather, who couldn't come to the hospital because he was caring for his wife, ill with cancer. He called to tell her that they loved them, and they were praying for them.

Her nine-year-old daughter called to say, "Give Daddy my love, and tell him I'm taking care of Joey."

She told me about their tenth anniversary coming up next month and the big surprise she had planned for him. She hoped that his back injury would be better so that he would be able to enjoy it.

When she went out, she always brought him back something; a huge, red, heart-shaped balloon lettered *I Love You*, a huggy bear, or a favorite snack food. She even came in with a huge basket of fresh fruit she offered to share with us.

God was showing me that my first impression had been all wrong; this was a lovely, caring, young wife and mother, whose fashion sense happened to be different than mine. But under it all, she and I were much alike. Two women who would sit by the hospital bed for hours so as not to miss the moment when the doctor might come in to ask questions and get straight answers about our husbands' condition and prognosis.

I thought I had learned long ago not to judge people by their appearances. God used this unusual young woman to remind me again that some of the most interesting books I have ever read had some really unusual covers. He also reminded me that He loves each one of us, no matter how strange we may appear on the outside. His love is great enough to encompass a gray-haired, overweight, old woman, as well as this young person, whose taste in outerwear was so different than mine.

As evening set in, the nurse came to tell me that a private room had become available. Howard would be moved there in a few minutes. She told me they would bring in a cot for me so I could stay with him through the night. The window overlooked the St. Lucie Inlet. The water was so calm, that it was hard to tell whether the lights sparkling on the surface were reflections from streetlights or if they were stars. Once again, the Lord knew our needs and provided for them with a brief timeout to remind me of a much needed lesson.

It was shortly after this experience that my husband went home to be with the Lord. Thanks to that young woman, I learned to look for the person who lives inside the skin. Now, if I meet a young person with a big, bushy hairstyle, jeans with holes in the knees and other places, I try to see that person as Jesus would, and I try to show them His love.

Looking back, I wonder if she could see Jesus in me. I pray she did.

THE STORY OF THE WEEPING WILLOW TREE

I always thought of a large, Weeping Willow tree, with its branches swaying gently in a summer breeze, as a lovely picture. The sight relaxed me.

When we went out to look at the house and I saw those trees, the big Weeping Willow in the back yard and the huge Box Elder in the front for morning shade, I knew I wanted to make that our home. There wasn't a garage, but Howard figured he could build one exactly like he wanted. There was plenty of room on the five-acre parcel of ground.

Then, when he found an area in the little patch of woods on the back of the land where deer had been bedding down, he too felt compelled to call this our home.

The deal was closed, but before we even started to move, he began laying the foundation for his thirty-six feet by thirty six feet garage. With the help of family and friends, it was up and closed in from the weather in no time. When we made the move, eighty percent of our belongings were stored in that garage for several months.

The original part of the house was twenty feet by twenty-four feet. The foundation was laid up in stones, and the joists were made of hand-hewn lumber. Someone had built a small bathroom on the north side, and later someone else had added another bedroom on the west side. Whoever did that could not compare with the workmanship of the original craftsman. At some much later date another addition, about twenty by forty was added on the south side. All in all, it made for a sizeable square footage for a house. It just desperately needed to be remodeled.

The timing worked out well for us. Howard had been working part-time for an employer who was a patient, understanding friend. He operated a small tool and gage shop and was able to use my husband's talents when the shop was quiet. Business was too slow; as a result the entire crew was laid off. Howard had applied to be ruled as "unemployable" for the Social Security Administration. It was not long after the layoff that the Administrative Law Judge ruled him unemployable due to his severe hearing loss so that he could draw his full benefits to retire at age sixty-two.

Now I was working and he was staying home. I loved the irony of it. It was also exciting, coming home in the evening to see what he'd been doing in the realm of homemaking. He tore down walls, built a new beam to support the new walls, and removed the five-foot Youngstown steel sink that had been the kitchen. He gutted the west bedroom and removed the wall in order to combine the space with the original kitchen to make a room twenty-four feet by twelve feet. He lined the walls with new cabinets, matching the plan I had drawn.

On weekend mornings, I enjoyed sitting out on the deck he had built on the west side of the house. There I could sit and sip coffee, watch the humming birds, and enjoy my willow tree.

It wasn't too long before I learned why it was call a Weeping Willow. The tree literally "wept," and anything that stayed under it for any length of time was soon covered with a dark, sticky goop. I also learned that willow trees tend to shed; cleaning up the branches which fell kept me busy. I learned to adjust.

One unbearably hot summer afternoon in 1988, I was watching the sky. Clouds were moving in all directions, their colors becoming darker and darker. The wind grew stronger.

"We'd better get to the basement, now!" Howard said.

We barely made it down the stairs when the roar sounded overhead. In a few minutes, we cautiously made our way back up. The house was still there, and so were the garage and the deck. Whew! That was close!

We looked out the front window at the neighbor's house across the road to see that their garage had collapsed as if a giant fist had smashed it. It was then that we noticed the big Box Elder was broken and laying across the road. Going to the back yard, we saw what was left of the Willow tree. The upper two-thirds of it had twisted off, and it was resting on the roof of the garage.

That was when we realized how we had been protected. The twister had hit the willow and as it jumped over our house, it had gently laid the top of the tree on the garage. Then it came back down to take the Box Elder in the front onto the neighbor's garage, and not a shingle on our house was gone.

After we had thanked God for our protection, we were faced with the cleanup operation. Our son came with his big chain saw to cut up the part of the tree which had been blocking the road. He then left to help some of his neighbors who also had trees down. A few days later, he came back to cut up the standing wood into firewood.

Howard and our son had been cutting down what was left of the willow. The stump was so thick they had to make cuts from both sides in order to cut it up. They were making good progress when I heard an irritated male voice express frustration. I looked out and discovered the saw had hit something and broke the chain. That was the end of the job for that day.

Another day, another chain, and it was try, try again. By cutting inches at a time, they were finally able to reach the center of the stump to find the problem. It was an old ax head and a length of chain right in the center of the stump, which was over forty inches thick.

We tried to count the rings to calculate how old the tree was, but soon figured that apparently when it was very young, the tree had forked about as high as a man's waist. Maybe someone, possibly a hundred years or more earlier, had been chopping the trees when his ax handle broke. Had he just laid the head in the fork, intending to come back for it later? There had to be a reason that the ax head and that length of chain were buried in the middle of that tree.

My curiosity made me imagine all sorts of scenarios, of why, when, how, and who was responsible for this odd thing.

Perhaps I am a philosopher at heart, as I try to find a lesson out of all of this. That ax head had to cause the tree distress. No, I'm not saying trees can feel. I'm not that far gone, yet. As the decades went by, the tree gradually grew up and around that ax head and chain, until they were completely buried—until the chain saw discovered them.

I tend to think that we can learn a valuable lesson from that ax head. When others hurt us, perhaps it's wiser not to allow that pain to chafe at us. Isn't it better if we let the hurts go and continue our lives until we have grown around the pains and aches and reach a point where they are completely buried and forgotten? Was the old ax head teaching us a lesson in forgiveness?

HIDE AND GO SEEK

When I was a little girl, my sister and I used to play *Hide and Go Seek*. It was easy to hide from her if we were outdoors. I would hide in places she wouldn't go, like in the doghouse, in the middle of the shrubbery, or even in a tree.

Inside the house, it was more difficult. Being older and bigger than me, she knew all of the good places, like behind the couch, under the bed, or in the closet.

One day I had a flash of inspiration. Mother was having company for dinner and she had brought out her best tablecloth. It was linen and large enough to cover the dining room table and drape gracefully down on all sides.

As my sister counted to ten, she hollered out, "Here I come! Ready or not!" I crawled underneath the table. Once in my hiding place, I pulled myself up as high as I could, certain that if I couldn't see her coming, she couldn't see me. Wrong!

She came directly to the table, lifted the corner of the cloth and said, "I see you. Now, you're it. You call that hiding?"

How many times in life do we do the same sort of thing? Perhaps it isn't as part of a child's game, but do we sometimes try to hide ourselves?

Some action we've taken, or perhaps something we should have done but didn't do, caused a wave of guilt to come over us. Guilt and shame combined to make us want to hide some dark secret.

Jesus is there, ready and waiting to lift up the corner of the cloth and to say, "I see you. I understand,

and I'll forgive you if you want me to. If I forgive you, will you forgive yourself?"

LESSONS FROM AN OLD FARMER

After he was widowed, my husband's grandfather lived with us for several months. He'd always been a farmer and was used to rising early in the morning, having a hearty breakfast, and then going to work in his fields.

My husband worked in a machine shop and had to be at work at seven a.m, so early rising was also a part of our life. The problem arose when the old gentleman's hearty breakfast time conflicted with getting my husband fed, his lunch packed, and off to work.

As soon as the door closed behind my husband, it was time to roust out the children, get them up and moving, dressed, hair combed, teeth brushed, fed, lunches packed and ready to dash out the door in time to catch the school bus.

Many mornings would involve a child in tears because she thought she looked "just awful," or panic times of missing one shoe, or when homework had disappeared. The cacophony was torture to Granddad's advanced years.

He would rise early, have coffee with my husband, and then head out to his garden until he saw the bus leave. Then he'd come into the house, wash up, and sit in the kitchen with me. That time became so precious to me.

I'd fix his breakfast and then we'd just sit and talk. Well, he'd talk and I'd listen. I learned so many wonderful stories of his childhood. One morning, he'd talk of his family history, and the next he's be very philosophical. Either way, it was fascinating for me to hear, and I tried to soak up everything he said.

One particular morning he'd been concerned about his garden. The soil was so hard, and he'd put a lot of fertilizer into it and worked it into the ground, watering every morning, but with no improvement.

"What we need," he said, "is a good, violent, electrical storm."

I was shocked. I could see no good from a storm like that.

"Sometimes, after the ground has lain fallow, and unproductive," he went on, "even if you can plant good seeds in it, they'll struggle just to grow sickly plants and a poor harvest. A good electrical storm helps. When the lightning hits the ground, it opens it up, and nitrogen from the lightning washes into it. Once the ground is open, the rain runs into the cracks and refreshes it. After one or two good storms, the ground is richer, so plants thrive better than before the storms."

That philosophy stuck with me. There are times when peoples' hearts can be like a garden. They may lay fallow and unproductive. Seeds can be sown and a feeble effort made to grow a crop with poor results.

There may be times when God has to allow a good electrical storm into our lives. It might be something emotional or financial or perhaps a physical tragedy. Whatever it is, it can hit us like a lightning bolt, opening the hard areas of our hearts and allowing the refreshing rain to flow in, making our hearts more receptive to His will in our lives.

Have your recently had an electrical storm in your life? If so, don't fight it. Submit your heart to Him, and allow His love to flow freely into and over your being. Then watch how your heart's garden can bloom and prosper.

MUSTANGS AND COW PONDS

When my oldest son was twenty, he was able to buy his dream car, which was the envy of all the boys his age.

It was a 1970 Mach I, Fastback Mustang, painted gold, with black racing stripes and black louvers on the rear deck. It had been the "Official Pace Car" for the opening of the *Irish Hills Raceway* in southeastern Michigan.

This car was made to be driven fast, and he was happy to oblige. Years later, I learned that he had been dubbed "King of Chilson Road" by his friends. Chilson Road was a two-lane blacktop full of many curves, hills, and dips. He set the speed record for those few miles of road.

He worked as a shop foreman for the tool and gage shop, which my husband operated. One day the young man found himself running late for a dentist appointment. Needless to say, he hurried home from work to shower and change first.

How can I delicately describe a cow pond for those who have never seen one? A cow pond is a relatively shallow depression, maybe three or four feet deep. Water would stand there in varying depths for most of the year.

On hot, summer days, the cows would stand or lie down in it, seeking relief from the heat. They would often respond to nature's call while they were there. You might say the pond and the soil around it were like an oversized pigsty.

I was heading home soon after my son had left and arrived at the cow pond to see the flashing, blue lights of the sheriff's patrol car. I glanced to my left to see a car upside down in the pond, all four tires in the air. Perhaps there were two to three inches of gold colored paint showing.

May first reaction was, "Somebody's got a real problem." Then I saw my son talking to an officer and I wondered why he was there. Suddenly, I grasped the situation. It was his car!

Concerned that my son might have injuries, the officer kept trying to make him lie down, with no luck.

"My mom is going to be coming through here, and I've got to be on my feet!" he told him.

It wasn't long before the tow truck arrived. Needless to say, the driver was less than thrilled that he had to wade into that pond to hook up the vehicle. Before long, he had the car upright and towed to the road. It was covered with black-green slime and the stench was horrific.

He asked the boy for the keys and was told they were still in the ignition and the doors were locked.

The window on the driver's side was down three or four inches. All of the others were closed.

We could only wonder how he was able to get out of the car.

Perhaps someday he'll tell me that part of the story. Until he does, I must accept the promise in Psalm 91:11. "For he shall give his angels charge over thee, to keep thee in all thy ways." (KJV)

God kept his promise that day!

FRIENDLY FIRE

My husband went into the army in August of 1944. After basic training, he was shipped to California where he went through training for desert warfare. When that was completed, he was put on a troop ship heading west across the Pacific Ocean.

He soon found himself in the Philippine Islands as a "replacement," an innocuous word which meant there had already been many casualties, men severely wounded and killed. As an eighteen-year-old, who was five foot six inches tall and weighing one hundred twenty pounds, he didn't exactly fit the description of a *fighting man*.

The military had done a good job of preparing him for what lay ahead. In spite of his size, he was able to walk up to a telephone pole on the ground, find the balance point, pick it up, and carry it away. It was no wonder that the thirty-caliber gun he carried didn't seem heavy.

Having grown up on a farm during the depression, he learned as a lad how to shoot and hit whatever he aimed at. His score at the firing range during training was so high he was presented with that heavy weapon. Some reward!

He was assigned to a unit comprised of men who had already seen combat since early 1942. Years later, at a reunion of the outfit, one man said he remembered "the skinny, little kid with the big machine gun" when he joined their unit.

My husband's first mission came as part of a squad, which was ordered to move up a narrow, winding road around a mountain. He described it as a "ledge" with the sides going straight up and straight down. Shortly after they began to move out, the enemy opened fire on the point men. There was little or no cover to protect them. At the head of the line were the radio operator and the man who carried the set. He quickly called for an air strike to provide covering fire.

Because he was carrying that machine gun, my husband was near the end of the long column of men. He said he heard the scream of the engines of the P-38 fighter plane as it dove to strafe the area. Unfortunately, the pilot mistook the American GI's for the enemy and made several runs, strafing the area before he was given the message to stop. It was a tragic mistake; they called it *friendly fire*.

Of course, the men all hit the dirt and did what they could to cover themselves. He told me later that the concussion of the bullets hitting the ground caused many of the men to bleed from their ears and eyes, and it forced the dirt into any uncovered skin.

The radioman and several others at the head of the line were severely injured and were taken away to a nearby field hospital, then shipped away for more care. Their friends felt certain they either were dead and dying. Those with less serious injuries were treated there and remained with the outfit.

When I think about this event, I cannot help but compare it to an all-too-frequent occurrence in our churches. Sometimes our leaders may face dark and desperate situations and call for help. Far too often that call is answered by "friendly fire."

I've heard it expressed that the church is the only group which attacks its own wounded. Isn't it sad that so-called "Christians" can be so cruel and will allow the enemy to use them as a weapon against leaders and other church members? We have an enemy who comes to kill, steal, and destroy; he is even in the churches!

So, if our pastors or those in leadership should be tripped and fall, what should our attitude be, when they show repentance?   If we consider our churches to be as hospitals there to help the sick and dying, should we consider them to be too fouled, too dirty, too messed up? Might we think they will contaminate our nice clean emergency rooms?

Or should we be ready to reach out to them in love, willing to accept, comfort and heal them? What would Jesus do? Remember how it was told in John 21:16 & 17; Peter had tripped and fallen, but Jesus forgave him and encouraged him to return to his ministry. Can we do less?

LOOKING UP AT THE DOCK

It was a beautiful July afternoon in northern Michigan. We were on Lake Charlevoix, where the north and south forks of the Jordan River meet and go on to empty into Lake Michigan. Our slip was in *The Narrows*, which was a snug harbor at the western end of the South Fork. From there we could easily access either fork or follow the channel out to Lake Michigan.

She was a thirty-foot Chris-Craft, pre-World War II model, which had been kept in pristine condition. Her name was *NiteCrawler*. Her previous owner gave her that name because his daughter said all they did with her was go out at night and crawl around the water.

This day, with our daughter and another couple aboard, we decided to slowly cruise down the large arm to its western end at Boyne City. There was a restaurant there we always enjoyed. It was within walking distance of the public docks. That's where we planned to have lunch.

We came into the slip easily. My husband had become quite comfortable handling the boat in different circumstances. As she neared the dock, I took the stern line in hand, jumped off the boat, ready to whip the line around the big cleat.

We'd done this operation many times with no problems, but this day the wind suddenly changed to come out of the north. Before I could make a loop around the cleat, the wind gusted. It blew the boat away from the dock, taking me with it.

I don't know how deep I was in the water; all I could think was, *don't let go of the line!* When the line went taut, I knew which way was up, so that was the direction I scrambled.

As my head broke the surface, I heard my friend screaming. "She can't swim! She can't swim!"

By now a crowd had gathered. Men were shouting their opinions of what to do next. My husband couldn't see that I had pulled myself up to the side of the boat. He worried that if he did as they told him, he might crush me between the sea wall and the boat.

My friend and her husband helped me back over the side. When my husband could see me, he calmly maneuvered the boat into the slip with no problem.

After he turned off the engines, many volunteers helped get the lines fast. They tried to get me to release the line, but no way! I had a grip on it and was not about to let it go.

Eventually, I did let go of the line and put on some dry clothes. We walked to the restaurant to enjoy dinner and then a casual stroll back to the *NiteCrawler*. The trip back to our slip was soothing and uneventful—really pleasant.

That night when we were alone in the cabin, I grabbed that line and cried and cried. I hadn't realized how frightened I'd been, but I did make a decision at forty-two years of age. I decided to learn to swim.

As I lay awake that night, I realized how fortunate I had been. I could have been seriously injured or drowned. But that line was in my hand. I owed my life to a piece of nylon rope and the grace of God!

Since that experience, I can fully appreciate the old gospel hymn, "Throw out the lifeline. Some poor soul may be drifting away." I thank God for that lifeline that day and the way my heart took the lesson. He is always there to save me—to throw me a line. Is He there for you?

BIG FAMILY, ONE BATHROOM

For several years when my older children were growing up, we had just one bathroom.

Two adults and three kids meant there were five different ways to handle a tube of toothpaste. My husband was a *squeeze in the middle* type. My system was to smooth out the tube and then try to keep the end rolled up neatly as the contents were used.

One son favored laying the tube on the counter, cap in place, and mashing down with his fist. Of course, when the cap was removed, toothpaste squirted everywhere.

One girl would only handle the tube if it were wrapped in tissue. She didn't want to be in contact with her brother's germs. The other girl would touch the tube daintily with one finger, holding her brush in place with the other hand.

Needless to say, just trying to keep the cap on the toothpaste was an ongoing battle. In conjunction with that struggle was the effort to get them all to clean up the counter top when they were finished.

Why is it that spilled-toothpaste wipes up so easily with a tissue when it's fresh? Yet when allowed to air-dry for a few hours, it nearly takes a chisel to remove?

These memories of long ago were triggered by a conversation I heard about a project that was used in a Vacation Bible School.

The teacher had given each student a tube of toothpaste and encouraged him or her to make a design on paper. Then she asked them to try to put the "goop" back into the tubes.

The moral of the lesson was that we should be careful of the words that come out of our mouths. Hurtful, angry words can pop out quickly. Even if we regret saying them, we cannot take them back; they just won't go back into the tube.

She explained that the situation could be easily cleaned up if we act right away to seek forgiveness. A "tissue" of *I'm sorry, I didn't mean that; please forgive me* can wipe it away.

The tragic thing is that often the hurtful words are allowed to "air dry," and as they harden, their target becomes angry, bitter, and spiteful.

But the grace of God is always there to touch each heart—both the wounded and the "wounder." His love and mercy are always ready and waiting to heal broken hearts and broken relationships.

In the same manner, He is always ready to forgive us when we ask for His forgiveness.

TRADING STAMPS

Sometimes when I mention S & H Green Stamps or Top Value Stamps, younger people look at me blankly. They have no idea what I'm talking about.

In the early years of my married life we had to watch pennies very carefully. One way I found to save money was to do my shopping at gas stations, hardware stores and grocery stores that gave *trading stamps*. S& H Green Stamps and Top Value Stamps were the most popular in our area. For every dollar spent, the merchant would give us a stamp worth perhaps ten cents on the dollar in exchange.

I took the stamps home and carefully pasted them in the book provided by the stores. When I'd have three or four books full, I'd go through the redemption catalogue to see what I could get in exchange for my full books.

In a city about forty miles from our home, there was a Top Value redemption store. I'd go there, clutching my filled books, to redeem them for some treasure our budget wouldn't cover. Perhaps I'd get a small appliance, a special toy for the children, or some piece of furniture, just for redeeming the books—no cash was needed.

A trip to the store was always an event, even more special when as many as ten or twelve books were involved.

With the coming of the *supermarket*, the trading stamp business became obsolete. It was an expense the smaller merchants could no longer afford.

I was talking with my son recently about those Top Value Stamp days, when he told me a true story.

He'd taken a job remodeling an old house. The building needed to be gutted from the attic to the ground level. In the process, he found an old trunk in the attic.

Curious, he opened it to see what treasure it might hold. He was amazed to see it packed full—top to bottom—of books of Top Value Stamps. He said there must have been several hundred completely filled books. What once had been a valuable asset years ago was now just junk—old paper destined to end up in a dumpster.

The company had long since gone out of business, so it was too late to redeem them.

I cannot help but wonder how many good, religious people there are who have been in church all their lives, have heard the gospel, and have even sung the *Old Redemption Story*, yet have never claimed it for themselves.

All of the good works they've done, all of the money or time they've given will be as worthless as that trunk full of Top Value Stamp books.

They've known about the Scripture promises for themselves made in Galatians 2:20. "I live by faith in the Son of God, who loved ME, and gave himself for ME!" (Words in all capitals are by the author for emphasis.)

BOYS AND THEIR TOYS

When I was first married I was so in love with my husband; I felt every other woman in the world must love him too. I was very insecure in his love for me. As time passed, I learned the difference between being in love and loving.

Loving isn't something we are in; it is something we chose to do. When I learned that lesson, I became more confident in our relationship.

As the years passed, I realized I would never have to be concerned about Howard being unfaithful to me with another woman. My concern was *machinery*! Any kind of machinery. It didn't matter if it went round and round, up and down, floated, or whatever; machinery was his second love. Of course, if one had machines, one also had to have tools to keep them running—every type of tool imaginable.

Being thrifty—or a scavenger, to be honest about it—he was always on the lookout for used items. His theory was that if one of something was good, two were better, and a third was even better; then he would have extra spare parts (just having spare parts wasn't good enough). Whenever he found a used whatever, he would disassemble the second one and save every part, bolt, and nut.

Never throw anything away; I may need it someday became his motto. As his collection grew, he had to have a place to store everything, so the next item on his wish list became a garage—a *big* garage.

My feminine nature was conflicted about this. All of this junk was a nightmare to live with. On the other hand, whenever something broke, he was right

93

there, ready, willing and able to repair it. He always had the right parts for whatever the need was. God even blessed him with the innate knowhow to repair anything.

As he would modestly tell you, "Anything some fool can put together, I can take apart and make it better than when it was new." That wasn't just idle boasting. He really could!

One time he came home with a big, old, Regulator clock, which they used in schools. It didn't work, but he got "such a good deal" on it. I shook my head and kept my peace. For several days my kitchen table, countertops, and every flat surface in the room were covered with hundreds of pieces of screws, springs, gears, and items I'd never seen before. One evening, he proudly called me to come see what he had done. The clock was working and the chimes rang on the hour and on the half hour. Of course, I had to be properly awed by his brilliance; I didn't even have to pretend.

Machines of any type always fascinated him. His real pleasure came from the many cars, boats, snowmobiles and motorcycles he had over the years. Early in our marriage, the cars came and went because they usually arrived in a state of disrepair. He would get them running right and looking better, and soon they'd be gone. They would be replaced by another one, which needed his tender, loving care.

It was sheer joy for me when the time came where he nurtured one to a healthy state and gave it to me to drive. I no longer had to take him to work about thirty-five miles away so that I could have a car to do my shopping, etc, and rush to be ready to make that thirty-five-mile trip to pick him up at the end of his shift.

Over the years, he also collected models of cars he had either owned or had dreamed of owning. He built model airplanes, ranging from a balsa wood model of a WW II P-38 Fighter Plane, to models that were radio controlled with wingspans of six-feet or more. After we moved to Florida, he enjoyed going out to the club where many men flew their planes and attending air shows.

When I asked him why he didn't try to fly his planes, he said, "Flying them is easy; landing them isn't. I couldn't stand to crash to pieces one I'd work so hard on."

After his death, it was necessary to get rid of all this stuff. As we cleaned out the thousands of parts, nuts, bolts, screws, etc, I had to laugh at the men who walked away carrying their new treasures, smiling to themselves at "such a deal" they'd gotten.

Their wives shook their heads and kept their peace. We were sisters under the skin; we understood each other. One lady told me that at their home in Port Huron, Michigan, the guys would say, "Don't go to Lowe's; go to Joe's." She told me this while her husband loaded the back of his pickup truck with several drawers filled with goodies.

I thank God for giving Howard mechanical abilities and the desire to salvage and repair whatever things would be in need of his talents. Having a handyman in the home was a blessing. It taught me many lessons in being a good steward, to waste not, because the Word tells us in Luke 16:2, that one day we will be called to give an account of our stewardship.

IS THAT YOU, PEDRO?

All the years of our married life, my husband wanted to have birds. Not canaries—he wanted birds that had beaks which could poke holes in human flesh.

His birds ranged from parakeets to budgies to a Blue Front Amazon. He admired a cockatoo and a macaw from time to time. When that happened, I did something I rarely did. I said, "No!"

One of his assorted, feathered friends was a Redheaded Conure named Pedro. He bought Pedro because he had heard him say, "My name is Pedro."

Pedro and I got along alright. We just ignored each other. He became attached to my husband, and even I could see there was a type of bond between them.

One January day, we planned a weekend getaway to northern Michigan to ride the trails on our snowmobiles.

Before we left, we had given our grown kids the house rules to follow while we were away.

1. Their married brother and sister would be making spot checks on them—unannounced.
2. No parties.
3. No tying up the telephone. When we'd try to call, the line must not be busy more than twice at any time.
4. Friends in the house were okay, but only if on the "approved" list.
5. Clean up after yourselves.
6. Do NOT take Pedro out of his cage.

97

When we returned home on Sunday evening, our married daughter's car was there, as well as our son's *approved* friend. We entered to find the house tidy, the young people laughing at a TV program, and Pedro in his cage. All was well.

Howard kept telling me there was something wrong with Pedro. He thought maybe the kids had scared him and he'd had a breakdown. He just didn't act right.

Winter passed and spring came. The kids did an inordinate amount of giggling and whispering. We knew something was afoot, but what?

As the weather warmed, one day I decided it was time to clean the side-by-side- refrigerator-freezer. There wasn't much in the freezer, so I defrosted the unit and sorted through the few packages left from the winter stock. Of course, I found a few containers of leftovers with no date and with freezer burns, which I tossed in the garbage.

One package was wrapped in white freezer paper with no marking. As I unwrapped it, suddenly all of the whispers and giggles made sense. There was Pedro!

As the story was related to Dad later that evening, the boy had taken Pedro out of the cage to show him off to the *approved* friend. Something spooked Pedro, and while the kids were trying to recapture him, the tomcat decided to join the fun. He was successful. Pedro went quickly, gone before the cat dropped him.

The married sister was involved too. She had called around and found a pet store about forty miles away, which had a Redheaded Conure, a ringer for Pedro.

The rest of the story is unimportant. Dad had to mete out justice, tempered with mercy. He was upset about losing his bird, but the conspiracy of silence and lies were what he punished.

The moral of this story is clear. We can try to cover up our wrongdoings, and for a while it will appear that we can get away with it. But it says in Numbers 32:23, "Be sure your sin will find you out!" (NKJV)

OUR TOWN CHARACTER

I guess every small town has its own "character." While reading Tom Bodet's "The Big Garage on Sure Shot," I was reminded of my hometown's character.

His name was Fred Server. Old timers said he was never right after he came back from World War I. Some even said he was a little strange before he went.

He lived with his father until he died; his mother had died many years before I became aware of him. I remember seeing him around town, always with no socks or coat, regardless of summer or winter. His trousers were always too large for him, held up by suspenders. He always wore long sleeve shirts, not buttoned at the cuffs.

He continued his father's business of buying junk and selling antiques. I never went in his house, but those who had, told of a place like a rabbit warren with rooms full of boxes and piles of strange items so jammed full that you could only walk through narrow pathways. His little house sat on the edge of Howell Lake just north of Mt. Olivet Cemetery and a couple of factories.

Everyone in town looked forward to winter and the lake freezing over. In addition to ice skating, the favorite winter sport was to go watch Fred cut two holes in the ice, several hundred feet apart. He'd dive into the first, swim to the second and surface there. He'd shake the water off and stroll back to his house wearing nothing but his shoes and his underwear.

Fred had a strange way of walking—sort of leaning forward from his hips and almost, but not quite running—kind of like the way Groucho Marx did, but slower.

One vivid memory I have of him was one summer afternoon in the late 1940's. I was sitting at the window of our second-story apartment, trying to catch a breeze, when he drove up in his old wreck of a car, something out of the early 1930's, and parked on our corner. He made that funny little run across the street to the A & P store.

He returned shortly carrying a big watermelon. Fred sat down on the running board of his car and threw the melon onto the curb. Of course, it broke into pieces, and he began picking up the pieces one by one and biting into the meat and then throwing down the rind. He continued until the meat was gone and the rind littered the curb. Then he stood up, wiped his hands on his pants, walked around to the other side of the car, got in, and drove away.

After I was married, I didn't see much of him, but my husband came home one night telling me he'd stopped in at Fred's house. He'd been trying to find some small part for something, and sure enough, Old Fred had it. He told me all about the long row of brass trumpets, used for speakers on early record players or Victrolas, as they were called, and many other oddities stored in Fred's house.

I don't know when Fred started letting his graying hair and beard grow, but I do remember seeing him one time when they were chest and shoulder length.

The last time I heard of him was a few years later. One Sunday, our church had a picnic at the city park near his home. Howard and I were sitting at a table with another couple, watching the children playing. Suddenly, their small son, about four-years old came running up to them.

"Mama, Daddy, come quick! He's here! He's here!"

"Who's here," we all chorused.

Just then Fred came into view, walking up the path toward the beach. His hair and beard had turned completely gray, and he was wearing some kind of old terrycloth bathrobe and sandals.

"See, Mama! See, Mama!" little Phillip cried. "It's the dear Lord! It's the dear Lord!"

Fred gently patted him on the head, smiled, and walked on without saying a world.

We adults laughed, but I couldn't help but think of my paraphrase of Mark 10:15. "Except you become as little children, you will not see the kingdom of heaven."

I don't know when he died, but the last time I was in Howell, there was a new "town character." I don't remember his name, but he went to school with my oldest son. He is a Viet Nam veteran. I saw him sitting cross-legged in raggedy fatigues in front of the bank with his hat in his lap.

I hope there will be some people who will treat him with more respect than my generation did Fred. Maybe someday a child will see the *dear Lord* in him too.

WHO NEEDS KIDS?

Only my husband and I were left at home now; the children were grown and gone. We had settled into a pattern of life that may seem dull to some. It worked for us and our critters: a small dog, a cat of gargantuan size, and a Blue Front Amazon parrot.

Ting, a ten-pound Lhasa Apso, was used to staying in her kennel when we went out. If she didn't head for it when I'd pick up my purse, all I had to say was, "Little house time," and in she went.

The cat, a Maine Coon, was named Pierre when we adopted him from the Humane Society, and he weighted over twenty pounds. He had a black, silky coat, white tips on his paws, a small, white blaze on his chest and a white mark on his lip that looked as if he had a milk moustache. He had the run of the house with two litter boxes and a pair of food and water dishes.

Joseph, the parrot, was named for his coat of many colors. He had two cages. One was his outdoor house on the screened porch, and another in a closet for his quiet times and when the Florida weather made the outdoors too chilly. He also had a perch with several toys by my husband's chair.

When my husband had to go into the hospital, I wasn't too concerned about the critters. I made sure they each had access to food and water. Ting had great bladder control, and the other two had their own facilities.

The system worked fine. As soon as I came home, I would let Ting out. Pierre followed along to make sure she did it right. After the outing, Ting got her treats and then I took off my shoes to get comfortable. That's the way it had been going until one night.

I apparently hadn't closed the cage door securely when I'd left. Joe escaped, and that's what started the games with the cat. I could see the path where the cat had dashed around the room, knocking things off the table, jumping on the back of the couch, then hopping down behind it, which caused the TV to come unplugged. All of this was done as he chased the bird around the house, up and down.

Ting must have felt left out, as she had scratched and tore at the two-inch foam pad under the blanket in her house until shredded foam was everywhere!

Facing the mess, I tried to decide whether to use the broom or the vacuum cleaner. I decided on the broom, not wanting to plug up the hose on the vac. It seemed like the more I swept, the more bits of foam I'd find. I'd move the kennel or a chair, and there was more foam underneath. I finally got the mess cleaned up and collapsed into my chair.

Down the hall, I heard a voice calling, "Howard. Howard." It was Joseph, letting me know it was his turn for attention. Now Joseph and my husband got along beautifully, but he and I got along only as long as there was a thirty-six-inch stick between us.

In order to clean his cage and fill his food and water dishes, I would get him on the stick and set him on Howard's bed, where he could walk around. He and I would keep our distance from each other. I took the dishes from the cage and headed for the kitchen.

Hearing a flap of wings beside me, I turned to see that he had jumped off the bed and was now on the floor following me.

This was the time for caution. I could not forget the time when I had gotten careless around him. The moment I turned my back on him, he flew and landed on my back, his needle-like talons digging through my sweater and into my skin. I had no desire to repeat that episode. But this time I was so tired I decided if he wanted to get rough, I would too. After all, this wasn't the first time he'd done this to me, he was a known repeat offender.

Walking down the hall to the kitchen, I kept one eye one him, ready for a fight. He boldly waddled the length of the hall, past the little dog, who sat and watched, and the cat that apparently also had learned to keep his distance. The bird watched as I washed and refilled his dishes. I fully expected him to do something.

Job 3:25 came to my mind. "That which I feared has come upon me." (NKJV). He surprised me by not doing anything but waddling back up the hallway. He hopped up on the bed, stepped onto his end of the stick, and sat there waiting for me.

I cautiously replaced the dishes and added a few treats. I reached for the stick, and he quietly sat there as I put him in the cage. Making certain the lock was secured, I reached for the light switch and said, "Goodnight, Joe."

I was stunned to hear him say, "G'night."

More of Job came to mind. "The beasts of the field will be at peace with you. You shall know your tent is at peace. You shall visit your dwelling and find nothing amiss. (Job 5:23-24 NKJV).

Don't we have a kind and loving God? He even uses the beasts in our homes to show us how much He cares.

A CHURCH CAMP FAMILY VACATION

In 1962 we wanted to take a family vacation, but our money situation was very tight. How do you find a solution for that problem?

We read that every year our denomination sponsored a Family Camp in north central Michigan. At this point, it's hard to recall just how much the cost was, but for Mom, Dad, and five kids, it was a very good deal. The literature told of individual cabins overlooking a lovely lake, people available to entertain the children of all ages, Bible study classes for the adults each day, and plenty of free time to enjoy games, boats, and other such fun things. Best of all to Mom, all meals were included!

Once we made the decision to take advantage of this blessing, it was time for all of the necessary planning: what clothes to pack, who would need what, toys to take for the children, etc. At this time our kids ranged from a thirteen-year-old girl to the baby girl, who was not quite one year old. In between them, were an eleven-year-old boy, an eight-year-old girl, and another boy of five.

Looking back now, I have a problem believing that I was able to manage the logistics of pulling this motley crew together, plus Dad and myself, along with all of the vital things and didn't forget anything or anyone. I even remembered to bring our own bedding and towels for the cabin, and the bug spray. Thank God for large cars with big trunks.

When we arrived at the camp on Monday morning, we were not disappointed at the grounds. They were indeed lovely. We unloaded the car and got settled in as other families began to arrive. About noon, the bell rang at the *Mess Hall* cabin, and we all made our way there with stomachs growling. The tables were long and arranged in a horseshoe shape. This was to encourage families to mix and get acquainted. We had a nice lunch of soup and sandwiches, beverages, and fresh fruit for dessert.

The best part of it all happened after we finished eating. I began to clean up after my family, and one of the staff came up to me and said, "Stop! You can't do that here. This is vacation for everybody— Moms included. You go outdoors and enjoy the view until the next bell rings that will call everybody to the chapel to tell you about our agenda."

I guess you know that I had no problem accepting that. As I wandered around, I was blessed by the scenery; the lake was a beautiful blue, the sky was gorgeous, and it was like a movie setting. The breeze coming in off the lake was fresh and smelled so good.

At about two o'clock the bell rang, and we all headed to the chapel. It was in an old barn, which had been swept clean, whitewashed inside and out, and had benches for seats. There was a small platform on which were located a piano, a couple of chairs, and a lectern.

The camp manager welcomed all of us and made the necessary introductions. There were five pastors and their families, and we were one of two laymen and their families. I had visions of having to be very pious for the next few days. That perception was quickly changed once the pastors relaxed and became "just folks."

The basic agenda was the same every day.

Breakfast from seven thirty to eight thirty.

Bible study was held in the chapel from nine thirty to eleven.

Lunch was from noon to one.

Then we had free time until five, when dinner was served.

Wednesday evening at seven p.m. we attended a brief church service.

The rest of the week remained the same except for Sunday morning, when we attended another church service at nine in the morning before heading home.

Other than that, we were free to do whatever we wished. They told us about the shopping in a nearby town, where the local theaters were, and what movies were playing, the bait shop for the fishermen, and local points of interest.

All the times when the adults and older teens were in chapel for anything, there were other young people to work with the younger children in crafts, Bible stories, etc. That week was so full, so exciting, I cannot begin to tell you everything about it.

One pastor led the morning Bible study in Galatians, and another led the Wednesday service. A third pastor took care of the Sunday morning service. Those were the only times one would guess they were pastors. As it turned out later, one of them was a ping-pong champion, and the others were not far behind him. My husband did himself proud in that area too.

As we became acquainted, we learned that one pastor and his brother, the other lay family, had grown up on the streets of a large city, where they learned, among other things, to play ping-pong with paddles without handles. The YMCA where they went didn't have any paddles that had handles. It was interesting as they told their story of their youth, the gangs, and how they worked in the nearby pickle factory to earn money for school.

My husband, the mechanic, always had a good assortment of tools in his car, and they came in handy when one brother's car wouldn't start on the first day of free time. Between the three of them, they got the needed parts, and got it running—not just running, but purring.

One pastor supervised, and when he saw my husband's timing light, he asked if he would check his engine too. Looking back now, I can see where my husband's talents and abilities were a ministry used of God even back then.

Every evening, there was a campfire around the base of a twelve-foot high cross. As we'd sit and watch the fire, listening to the night sounds, someone would begin to sing an old gospel song. Soon the whole group sang in harmony. It wasn't long before the moms would take the younger children into their cabins to settle them into bed. Not long after that they would rejoin the circle. It was a time of peace and fellowship like I'd never had before. Even old married couples like us could be seen holding hands or in each other's arms.

The children had a lot of fun. On Saturday, the youth counselors had a "shoe kicking contest." They were divided by ages, told to stand on a mark, and then kick hard to see how far they could send their shoe flying. My four oldest took first place in each of their age groups. I smile every time I think of the pictures of that.

There are many happy memories of that vacation, but there is one very special one, which I will always treasure. In that old barn chapel, high up on the gable end, the builders had cut a hole for ventilation to be used in the days when hay was stacked in the loft area. The hole looked to be about twelve inches across from where I stood on the floor, but it might have been bigger. On either side of that hole six or seven arrows were embedded in the wood.

One of the pastors used those arrows and that hole as a good setting for a message. His sermon reminded us that we could easily see those arrows, the ones that missed the mark. However, we had no way of knowing how many arrows had gone through the hole.

His point was this; God wants us to keep on trying. Every time we try and fail, every step we take when we falter in our walk, each mistake we make, and every failure is going to be apparent to others who are watching. We cannot succeed in anything unless we keep trying. The embedded arrows show the world our failures, but God is looking on from a different perspective. He no longer sees those arrows which fail. He only sees the arrows that went through the hole.

We don't have to concern ourselves about what the world thinks of us because we are forgiven by His grace and mercy. God only sees those arrows which clear the hole.

A RED TRACTOR

When we began having our babies, they came along at a regular rate: 1949, 1951, 1954, and 1957. We thought we were over that phase of our lives, when without warning we learned that we were going to blessed with a fifth child in 1961.

In those days, Dr. Benjamin Spock was considered to be the world's expert on childrearing. One would think every young couple in the world had read his book. It was the subject of conversation wherever young parents gathered. I had his book, and it was well worn in several areas. He made a big deal over the importance of coping with sibling rivalry and the problems it could create if children were separated by several years in age.

So when baby number five was on her way, I was concerned child number four would be jealous and create problems. In retrospect, I understand that if he was going to be jealous, there was nothing I could do to change it. If he were going to cause problems, he would do it, even if there weren't a baby number five.

Dr. Spock hadn't taken one particular thing into consideration; we had a *live-in love person*—my husband's grandfather. He spent hours with my little guy, telling him stories and encouraging him to gather up all of the ladybugs which had nested between my kitchen windows and put them in jars. I can only guess at the things that old gentleman told him. He was only four and a half when the baby was due. I hope he has some memories of those hours with that dear old man.

As summer passed and the baby's due date neared, I had packed the proverbial bag to take to the hospital. I would sit and talk to my little guy, telling him that one night soon I would go to the hospital and bring him back a baby brother or a baby sister. I would extol the virtues of having a baby in the house and how much I would need him to help me take care of it.

I asked him if he would rather have a brother or a sister, and without even thinking, he replied, "I'd rather have a big, red tractor."

As a good Dr. Spock mother, the next day I went out and bought a red tractor about twelve inches long and nine inches high and packed it in my suitcase so I wouldn't forget it.

This pregnancy was unusual in that it lasted ten months. My nerves were shot. Everyone in the family watched me as if I were a bomb about to explode.

Not my little guy. Maybe once a week or so he'd ask me, "When do I get my red tractor?"

Time changes all situations, and eventually the little girl did arrive, and the red tractor came home with her. He was thrilled with the tractor and couldn't have cared less about having a baby around.

Thank God for that live-in love person. This gentleman, almost ninety years old, would sit by her bassinette by the hour, and if she so much as squeaked, he'd jiggle it back and forth until she stopped. He didn't go so far as to offer to change diapers or feed her, but oh, the blessings of a non-fussing baby.

The moral of the story is this: my little guy was much like most of us adults. When God has something special or really wonderful He wants us to have, too often we cannot get our eyes off of the red tractors of the world. Will we miss His blessings?

Let us lift up the eyes of our hearts to see beyond the red tractors of this world and look for the blessings God has in store for us.

NEW EYEGLASSES

When our middle daughter was in the third grade, the school system began a new program of vision screening. After she was tested, the school called me to come into the office.

With two older children, I was not unduly surprised by the invitation. Usually, the calls were in regard to her older brother, but this was a new angle.

The day of the appointment, I went to the school, prepared to hear that she had done something to get into trouble. Imagine my surprise when the teacher said, "Oh, no! She's a good, little girl. I enjoy having her in my class. That's not at all why I called you."

She went on to explain the vision screening program to me and told me that they had discovered just how poor her vision was. The school would set up an appointment for the two of us to go to the University of Michigan Hospital for more testing. Of course, I agreed.

As we drove home that day, I asked her why she hadn't told me she couldn't see things. Her explanation was very simple: she didn't know she couldn't see things.

As the time passed while waiting for the appointment date, I began to notice the way she would squint when she tried to read a book, and why she always had to sit close to the television. I'd remember the times when I would point something out to her, and she'd say, "I can't see it. Show me where it is." I assumed she just wasn't looking in the right place. I had

119

guilty feelings, thinking that a good mother would have noticed and had done something about it.

It took several appointments to the clinic for tests and fittings before she was able to pick out a pair of glasses for herself. When she left the fitting room and came out to the waiting room, she climbed up on top of a bench to look out the third-floor window.

"Mama, I can see our car!" she exclaimed. "I really can see our car!"

Of course, I was in tears when another mother came up to me and told me about her little boy and his first glasses.

"It was winter when Tommy got his first glasses, and when we were driving home he cried and cried. I asked him why he was crying, and he replied, 'Because the trees are all broken.'"

She said it had never occurred to her before that he was only able to see the trunks of the trees; he had never seen the bare branches before.

On our trip home my girl kept reading aloud all the road signs, which she'd never seen before. It was early spring, and the trees were just leafing out. The sight of green leaves caught her attention, as she *oohed* and *aahed* over them. After we arrived home, she was thrilled to be able to stand on our front porch and see our cat hiding by the neighbor's fence about one hundred feet away.

Our vision is just one of the many wonderful gifts God has given us. It's so easy to take it for granted. As we get older, our physical vision can wane so slowly that we don't even realize how bad it's getting until it's almost too late to correct it.

Let's think for a moment about our spiritual vision. Do some of us need to go to "God's Eye Clinic" to be tested? If we did, would we be startled to realize how much of His plan for our lives we have missed? How we have been unaware of the greatness of His love for us. If we pray and ask Him to open the eyes of our heats to see Him in all His glory, He'll do just that!

LEARNING TO DRIVE

When I was about fifteen my mother wanted to teach my sister and me how to drive. I was gung-ho for the idea, but my big sister wasn't even interested.

We lived in a small town with relatively few cars on the road. One Sunday afternoon, Mother loaded us up in her car and drove out into the country to a side road, which she thought might be a safe place to begin with me.

She pulled over to the side of the road and got out, telling me to get out too. I'd been in the middle of the seat, and my sister sat by the passenger door. I did as I was told, then Mother slid in. I was right behind her, trying hard not to giggle.

Mother went through a long spiel about the gas pedal, the brake pedal, and the clutch pedal, and what each one was for. Her car had a *fluid drive*, which meant it could be driven without using the clutch. What a brilliant idea. I wondered if one didn't need to use the clutch, why was it there? I had sense enough not to ask, though. I could see she had already tensed up.

I started the engine, gently put it in gear, and ever-so-softly touched the gas. We didn't move.

"Give it some gas," she said, so I did. We moved too fast!

"Let up! Let up!" she screamed.

By this time the car wandered right and left a little bit as we rolled down the road. Alright, I confess; I was not keeping the car going in a straight line.

"Stop!" Mother screamed again. "Let me out! I'll drive!"

So I stopped. I figured that would be the end of my dreams of driving a car, at least for a very long time.

However, we hadn't taken into account the fact that soon, a young man would enter my life, and he would be very happy to teach me to drive *his* car. This pleased Mother too, and we used *his* car for the lessons.

It was good that he taught me to drive before we were married. If he had waited, he probably would have given up on me too, but at that time, he was still very patient with me.

I thought I would never get the hang of operating the clutch pedal and the gas pedal smoothly. I would either rev the engine so high that it would scream almost as loud as he yelled, "Let up! Let up!" or I would go by jackrabbit starts and stops, nearly giving both of us a whiplash injury.

When I was home alone I would sit by the window of our second-story apartment and watch people as they came to a stop for the traffic light, observing them smoothly driving away. I thought if they can do it, I should be able to do it too. Sometimes I'd sit in a chair and practice moving my left and right foot, coordinating their movements—left food down, right foot up, then left foot up, right foot down. Easy. Easy.

We struggled through this battle all winter, and then came spring, with soft roads and softer shoulders. Howard was driving somewhere—I don't remember where—when he pulled off onto the shoulder of the road.

He got out and said, "I want you to drive. I hear the rods rattling, and my foot is too heavy. You drive. Oh yes, be careful or you'll get us stuck in the mud."

I had no idea what rattling rods and heavy feet meant; all I could think of were his words, *you'll get us stuck in the mud.* I became so absorbed in not getting stuck, I didn't think about left foot, right foot, and surprisingly I was able to drive away smoothly with no jerking, no high revs, and no getting stuck.

I was so proud that I wanted to practice stopping and going the rest of the day. He humored me and let me do it a few hundred times before he took back the keys.

Through the years, I've learned that when we try to do something new, we make it a harder thing than it really is. We spend our energy thinking of the negatives in our life and have little energy left to get the job done.

When God has given me a job to do, I know now that if I just follow His leading and not ask questions like how, why, and what, He will help me get the job done.

I love the old song, *Where He Leads, I Will Follow.* Whether the road is smooth or muddy, straight or crooked, I'll go with Him all the way.

GRANDMOTHER, MEET PATSY...

I know I loved him long before I ever met him. As a lonely teenage girl, I would often sit by the window of our second-story apartment and watch people go by. I had seen him working at the Chevrolet garage across the street, and again as he drove around town in his beautiful 1942 Ford Coupe.

In the days of 1947, any car made in 1942 was practically new. His was black, and he kept it shining and the chrome polished. It looked good, and he didn't look half bad himself.

I would watch as he drove around, and I'd daydream about this handsome young, Prince Charming, and how someday he would come and "take me away from all of this."

One day later in the winter of that year, he suddenly stopped driving around, and my dreams went down the tubes. Well, so much for my handsome Prince Charming.

I continued plodding along in my boring life. While my sister dated a lot of different guys, and my mother even went on dates, I stayed home.

One Saturday, August fourteenth of that year, my sister had a date with a cute guy. His friend wanted him to fix up a blind date with me. He'd told him that I was the girl he was going to marry. So now her date wanted my sister to help him fix up a blind date for the two of us. She asked me, and I said I didn't want to go anywhere. I'd been cleaning house all day, looked a sight, and was just too tired. She coaxed and coaxed, and I finally gave in—just to keep peace in the family.

That evening when her date showed up, he escorted both of us down the stairs to his car and introduced me to his friend. I nearly fainted. It was my Prince Charming! You can guess the rest of the story.

As it happened, he'd been in a terrible accident and had been healing during the time he had disappeared.

Six days later, he took me out to meet his grandparents, who were basically the people who raised him. I was nervous about this, but he kept telling me to relax, that they would be nice to me.

As he drove up to the house, they were coming in from their garden. She had on a worn-out housedress, an apron, practical shoes, and a huge straw hat. She carried a basket full of fresh tomatoes, and perspiration ran down her face.

He took me to her and said, "Grandmother, this is my Patsy."

She set her basket down, opened her arms to me, and said, "Welcome, Patsy."

I went into her arms and I knew I was home.

His grandfather came along right behind her, and extended his hand to me. "Pleased to meet 'cha," he said. Again, I knew this was where I was supposed to be.

I always believed there was a plan for our lives, and I knew that Howard was the person I was meant to be with. I didn't know until years later that God said He knew us before we were formed in our mother's womb or that He had plans for us—great and mighty things, which man could not imagine.

I thank God that He gave me the sense to recognize what was right for me, and that I didn't let it get away.

LOOK FOR ME

I met her in 1947. Her husband was my husband's best friend. Over the years we grew close—almost closer than sisters.

Our children grew up with her son, and they felt as if they were cousins. Our families had picnicked together and played together; the boys were in Little League together, and the children had gone to school with each other. It was a great friendship.

One special thing we shared was the first day of school. Each year when school opened, she and I headed to the nearest shopping mall. We rarely bought anything. That wasn't important. It was the freedom—the liberation from being with the children 24/7.

We tried on hats, laughing at ourselves while the clerks looked impatiently at us. We might have lunch at the drugstore counter. We might buy the practical thinks like more pencils and paper or perhaps a forgotten but needed pencil case, or the like. Money wasn't plentiful, but it wasn't really necessary.

We started a tradition, which lasted until our sons eventually graduated from high school. To wind up our day of escape, on the way home we would stop and each have a banana split and giggle as if it was one hundred proof alcohol. In fact, after one such escapade, we were pulled over by a state patrolman, who wanted to know if we'd been drinking!

He hadn't complained about erratic driving, but he said he couldn't help but notice how much we were laughing. When we explained about the ice cream, with chocolate and marshmallow stains on our blouses as evidence, he laughed too. Then he waved us on our way. He said he was going to tell his wife about our tradition. She needed it too.

I didn't think she and I could become much closer; then her husband died in 1985. She'd had a mastectomy about a year prior to that, and the doctors had given her a clean bill of health. It wasn't long after his death on one of her regular trips for a checkup, she was given the bad news.

The cancer had come back and had spread to her liver. The doctor wanted to do more chemo, but she said, "No. I've had enough of that. I want to be able to enjoy whatever time I have left."

I could write several thousand words about the time we shared and enjoyed after that. She was blessed to have time with her little granddaughter, the one she'd always wanted to have.

She reached the point in her life where a relationship with the Lord was a vital to her as mine was to me.

One day, not long after she began to rapidly slip away, she took my hand, looked me in the eye and said, "It's been good, hasn't it? We've had a good life, haven't we?"

At a time like that, words don't express what is in your heart. The way she squeezed my hand in hers, and I squeezed back, said more than any words could.

"I'm going to leave you, but when you come along, I'll be just inside the gate, waiting for you. Look for me. I'll be there.

A few days later as I held her hand, she did go along; she slipped away with her dearly loved five-year-old granddaughter, Sarah, curled up beside her. Her parents had given the girl permission to be there.

After checking her heart and respirations, the hospice care nurse said, "She's gone."

"Is that all?" Sarah asked. "I thought it would be something scary." She hopped off the bed, waved goodbye and ran off to school. Her attitude was so mature and accepting. I think it helped her parents deal with the loss too.

I thank God that I had her as a friend and sister in the Lord nearly forty years. That was about twenty years ago, and recalling the experience, I must thank God for blessing me with a friend such as her. I treasure each memory of the time with her, and now, as I am gaining fast on my eightieth birthday, I look forward to the day when it will be my turn to go home.

When I get there, I will see Jesus first, and then my husband and I know I'll find her just inside the gate. She promised me she'd be there, waiting for me.

ARE THEY GOLDEN OR RUSTY?

They say these are the golden years, but some days I wonder if perhaps they're not just rusty. We develop aches and pains in places we forgot we had, and our social life revolves around doctor appointments.

My husband began to develop weakness in his legs, and it was my eye doctor who suggested the possibility that some of his medication might be the cause of it. When I called the cardiologist, he said to have him stop taking the medicine, and if it didn't improve in a few days to get him into the office.

From that day on, his health turned into a headlong rush downhill. The weeks flew by as they did one test after another, and it was plain to see that he was getting weaker every day. They put him in the hospital for more tests, and we all wondered if he would live until Christmas.

His many problems were too long to list, ranging from disintegrating discs in his spine, heart disease, diabetes, and now he'd gone into kidney failure.

Fortunately, all of our children were able to fly or drive to Florida to spend a few days with him. It was a time of healing and reconciliation, which was sorely needed.

He was in dialysis for over three weeks with no sign of regaining his strength. Who knew what the days ahead would hold for us?

We could only lean on God's Word. Paul wrote to the Romans in Chapter 4:16-18, *"We do not lose heart, but though our outer man is decaying, yet our inner man is being renewed day by day. For this momentary, light affliction is producing for us and eternal weight of glory far beyond all comparison, while we look not at the things which are seen, but at the things which are not seen; for the things which are seen are temporal, but the things which are not seen are eternal."* (NKJV)

Yes, those were days of wearing out and rusting and soon it was time for Howard to leave us and go home. What a wonderful future we have to look forward to when we have the *Golden Eternity*! Thank you, Lord!

AVERAGE? ABOVE?

In September of 1981, my pastor suggested that I attend a Speakers' Training seminar geared to help Christian women learn to share their faith. It was to be held at the Boy Scouts of America Camp near Brighton, Michigan, where Patsy Clairmont and her family lived. The speaker was a woman named Florence Littauer, author of several books. Her latest was, *It Takes So Little to be Above Average.*

The cover photo of that book was of several brightly-polished, Red Delicious apples. They surrounded a single, Golden Delicious apple, with just the right amount of red blush on its skin. This, of course, made it above average. Her goal was to help us to become above average women of faith, preparing us to share our faith in front of groups of people.

Florence is a tall woman with poise and glamour, hair coiffed just so, and make-up applied beautifully. She had been a teacher, and when she married John Littauer, their wedding was featured in *Life* magazine. She was a lady with whom I thought I had little or nothing at all in common.

When the ladies assembled, she had an assortment of items laid out on a table in the back of the room. There were fly swatters, clothes pins, rubber balls, sieves, pinecones, yardsticks, pin cushions, and other such varieties of common whatnots.

She asked each of us to pick one object and keep it with us until later in the day. I chose a large pinecone about four to five inches high and three to four inches in diameter. It had opened up in the warmth of the room. After the first session, we took a break and were scratching our heads over why we had these objects, and just what she expected us to do with them.

When we reassembled, she announced that our exercise would be to speak for two or three minutes on the item we had chosen, relating it to our faith. What could one say about a pinecone?

With my usual stroke of luck she called on me first. So there I was, standing in front of twenty-five ladies who were as baffled as I was. I had to give a short talk on a pinecone. My mind raced somewhat like the wheels of a locomotive on a greased rail, spinning like mad and going nowhere.

Simply standing next to Florence intimidated me. She stood about five-foot-eight-or ten inches tall, looking like a model. There I was five-foot-two in slacks and tennis shoes, no makeup, and with not much of a hairstyle. I was just barely out of my "house mouse" phase, and my knees played a wild dance. My hands shook and my stomach was full of at least a hundred butterflies. She gave me a formal introduction, and then I was on my own.

Holding the pinecone out in front of me, I kept looking at it and finally spoke out. "I guess I'm a lot like this pinecone. I'm short and round with some very rough edges. As this pinecone has opened up to drop its seeds, I like to think that I too am open to new things, new ideas, and maybe to drop some seeds along the way.

"God has made both of us, designed both of us to do a specific job, which He has planned for us. The verse in Ephesians 2:10 says 'We are His workmanship, created in Christ Jesus for good works, which God

138

prepared beforehand, that we should walk in them.' (NKJV) That verse has always meant a lot to me, as it promised that my life did have a purpose, a plan, and that I was not just an accident of birth."

I cannot remember the rest of what I said, but I closed saying that if God can use a simple pinecone, He can use me, if I am willing to let Him.

Then Florence put her arm around me and said, "It takes so little to be above average. Just see what you were able to do. You will be able to reach women that I never could because you are just yourself, nothing artificial."

The ladies gave me much encouragement by clapping. As I went back to my seat, my knees were still knocking and my hands were still shaking. There were still butterflies in my stomach, but now I think they were flying in formation.

Since then, I have been blessed to be able to speak to many women's groups, from eight or nine to as many as seventy-five or more. I can tell them how God has moved in my life, and how He can do the same for them if they will let Him.

I have been asked to teach many different classes, and have always replied that I am not a teacher. I can lead a discussion and encourage others to express themselves and to be open to new ideas. I have learned that when I prepare for a Bible study, I am able to share with others what I've learned. I am well aware of my limitations, but I've learned to trust God to lead me in the way He wants me to go, and He does.

TO PROTECT AND SERVE

When I was about twelve or thirteen, our town was so small we only had two police officers. The Chief was a skinny, little guy who strutted around in his uniform. He wore a double-breasted jacket, dark blue, and buttoned to the neck; his trousers were what we called *jodphurs*. They were flared at the thigh, and then narrowed at the knee and tight down his legs. He kept them tucked inside of his riding boots, always polished to a tee—all topped off by his Officer's cap.

Evenings he would park the only patrol car on the main four corners, and watch the goings on, which usually wasn't much. For those times when he decided to go somewhere, the town rigged a small, white, light bulb on top of the traffic signal. Situated there, if it were on, it could be seen for several blocks in all directions. I never knew who manned the telephone. If a call came from someone needing an officer, someone at the phone company switchboard would throw a switch and the light would turn on. When he saw that, he'd go back to the office to get the message.

As youngsters we looked at him as a comic relief. Sometimes I think Barney Fife was patterned after him, except Barney didn't look quite as silly. Years later, we saw a movie named *American Graffiti* in which some young people chained the police car to a lamppost. When they tried to drive it away, the rear axle came loose. The youth in our town didn't have that same success, but the squealing of the tires as the car tried to move did echo through the night.

When he left for the night, the other officer came on duty. His job was to walk the business district, all three blocks east and west, and two blocks north and south. He would try every door, and if it wasn't locked, he would go to the pay phone and call the owners. They might come and lock it, or just tell Walt not to worry about it; they'd wait until it was time to open.

If my sister and I went to the movies, we always had to go to the early show, which started at seven o'clock in the evening. That way, we'd be out about nine and have enough time to walk home before the curfew siren would blow.

That siren served multiple purposes. Seven nights a week at ten sharp, it would sound for curfew. Everyone under sixteen years of age had to be home unless they were with a parent. It also blew in the event of a fire to call all the volunteer firemen from their homes or jobs. They would hurry to the firehouse, get the location of the fire and away they went, sirens on the trucks screaming all the way.

It blew if a big storm was sighted, but the most memorable time it blew was on VJ Day, August 14, 1945, the day the war ended. It blew for over an hour as the town folk gathered at the main four corners. People in their cars drove up and down the main street, nylon stockings flying from the radio antennas, rolls of toilet paper waving in the air. One gal even had a box of Ivory Snow (a soap used to wash delicate things), shaking it in the air. Sounds strange now, but then gas, tires, stockings, soaps and many food items were rationed and worth their weight in gold.

Church bells tolled as the churches filled with people. August 14, 1945 was a day to celebrate, a day to remember. That night, the curfew was waived, and people of all ages were still in the streets late into the night.

Walt, the night watchman, was easy to like, not like the Chief. Everyone respected Walt. When we went to the movies and walked home, he was always walking about one block behind us to be sure we were safe.

I recall seeing him standing in the dark corner of the alley across the street from our apartment for several nights. I didn't think too much about it until one night when he caught a man who had climbed the back stairs to our apartment. He had been trying to open the door. My sister and I both slept right through the incident. We didn't know about it until a few days later when Mother told us about it.

When I remember Walt, I think of Psalm 91 (NKJV), where God promises us "no evil will befall us, or come near our dwelling place; to keep us safe, to give His angels charge over us."

Thank you, Lord, and Walt too.

PERSPECTIVES

When we were first married in 1948, we, like most people our ages, had to scrimp and save to get by, much less get ahead. Every month when we paid our rent, my husband dreamed of the day when we could have our own home.

In those long ago days, building requirements were not as strict as they are today. We drove through the country roads and saw places where people were building homes here and there. There were no big subdivisions in our part of the country. We could read about places like Levitt-Town, Pennsylvania, where a developer bought up a lot of vacant land and filled it with reasonably priced homes.

I think it was about 1950 when development began in a town about ten miles from where we lived. We drove over to look at the houses, and we were both disappointed at what we saw. Howard grumbled that there weren't any basements, and when he sighted down walls, he could see that they were not plumb.

"Lousy workmanship," he said.

I didn't like them because they had high, open ceilings; they called them "cathedral ceilings." They weren't that way just in the living room, but throughout the entire house. The walls, which divided the rooms, didn't reach to the ceilings; they were only eight feet tall. All I could think of was the sounds of crying children echoing through the entire building, or the noise of a TV keeping the children from going to sleep.

The more we thought of a home of our own, the more we decided to try to build it ourselves. It was not uncommon then for people to put in a basement and live in it while building the house above it.

We found a farmer who sold us one acre of ground on his farm for the grand sum of one hundred dollars. Sounds cheap now, but then our weekly income was about thirty dollars a week.

In the spring of 1951, we dug the footings and laid the blocks for a basement. We managed to get it closed in, sealed against the weather, and moved into our home just before Christmas that year.

It wasn't anything grand, but it was ours. The windows were tiny, sixteen inches high (a little more than the height of two cement blocks), and thirty-two inches wide (two and a half blocks long), so they didn't let in a lot of light.

We were enjoying our new life, when one spring day our oldest girl let out a blood-curdling scream. Pointing to one of the windows, she continued screaming. I couldn't move fast enough to stop the third scream. When I got to her, I looked out the window; looking back at us was a big, Jersey cow with her nose pressed against the glass.

I must be honest and admit that for a moment I was startled too, until I realized just what kind of monster was peeking in at us. After calming her, I took her outdoors and walked around to where the cow stood.

"Oh, it's just a moo cow!" she exclaimed.

Isn't it amazing how things and situations change appearance when we change the way we look at them? When we are at the low point, looking up at the problem, it can appear frightening and insurmountable.

When we get up, walk around, and look at them from a different perspective, they shrink in size.

When we have problems, we should claim the promise made in Galatians 4:6. "You are fully adopted as His children. . . crying out, 'Papa? Father?'" (THE MESSAGE)

He wants to show us how unimportant worldly things are in the perspective of eternity. Where would we feel safer than in our daddy's arms?

THE QUICKENING

We were married June 25, 1948, and as we began our new life together, we had much to learn about each other and each other's families. Not always fun. One thorny spot arose as the holidays approached; where would we spend Thanksgiving and Christmas—at his mother's or mine?

A compromise was reached. We would spend one with his family and the other with mine. Deciding which was which may lead to hard feeling, but we did the best we could.

One Sunday soon after Christmas, we were having dinner with his grandparents when Grandmother looked at me and asked, "When is the baby due?"

"What baby?" I replied. The thought of a pregnancy hadn't entered my mind until then.

"You have the look," she said. "Probably late summer or early fall, is my guess."

It wasn't long before I began to suspect she was right. No, I knew she was right. You've heard of morning sickness; well, I had morning, noon, and night sickness for about three months.

Life went on as usual in all other ways. As spring approached, the men all began talking about going smelt dipping up near Tawas. I had no idea of what or where Tawas was, and the idea of standing on the bank of a river in the cold, trying to dip out a fish, was the last thing I wanted to do.

It was April 19, 1949, when my husband and his buddy decided to on take this exciting adventure. My friend and I packed lunches for them, waved goodbye, and settled down at her house to spend the evening and night where it was warm and comfy.

As it got late, she made a bed for me on her couch, and she went to bed too. As I lay there, I had the strangest sensation; something moved in my stomach—actually moved!

I had been reading all of the "how-to" books, and I knew this sensation was the sign of a new stage of growth for the unborn infant. I lay there, giggling, and thinking about the baby who was growing inside of me. Overwhelming!

The rest of the smelt-dipping story is not important. I had a hard time waiting to see his grandmother to tell her about what I had experienced.

When I told her, she gave me the most marvelous hung, and said, "Patsy, that's the quickening! The Lord put life into your child!"

I treasure the memory of those next few months. All of the sickness was worth the joy and love I felt for this child.

She arrived on September 17, 1949—a beautiful little girl. Her daddy and I were all taken up in her. At one point, a man told my husband he would give him a brand new Ford and five thousand dollars for her.

"Oh," Howard replied. "I couldn't do that. The next one might not be as pretty." He was only joking, and I knew it, but he was right; the next one wasn't.

On the day in 1976 when I committed my heart to the Lord, I remembered that spring day in 1949. That day my soul and spirit were "quickened;" the Lord put new life into me, and I was changed, never to be the same again.

CORNFIELD GAMES

It amazes me how there can be several children raised in one family, and they all can be so different from one another—different likes and dislikes, talents and abilities, physical shapes and sizes, hair and eye color, dispositions and moods.

Our middle child, a girl, was and still is a person unto herself. She has the type of personality which is never daunted from trying anything. When her brother made a tree house, he hung a heavy rope to use for access and hung a sign, *no girls allowed*. That was all the motivation she needed to learn how to shinny up the rope when his back was turned.

When she graduated from high school, she wanted to go on to college, but my husband told her if she wanted to do that, she'd have to earn the money herself because he just didn't have the money to send any of his girls to college.

Long story short—she did just that. She earned her nursing degree, and Howard nearly popped his buttons when she showed him that she was now a Registered Nurse. Life went on; she married, and raised a family. More life changes came and she even became a grandmother, but her dream was still there.

It took her thirty-one years to accomplish that life goal. She received her Bachelor's Degree in Nursing.

But I'm ahead of my story. One time when she was little, she and a group of other youngsters were playing games in the cornfield across the road from our house. It had been very rainy, and the ground was muddy in the low spots. As she ran through the field, she lost one of her shoes in the mud.

When she came home to report the lost shoe, I reacted about the way a harried mother of five would; I didn't hesitate to yell at her, to let her know I was very upset about her losing a shoe, and dwelling on how much it would cost to replace it.

With voice at high pitch, I sent her back into that cornfield to find it, instructing her not to come home without it. If she'd been a different personality, she might have dissolved into tears and slipped away, but not this one. She spun around, kicked off the remaining shoe, and back into the field she went. She was not about to have me tell her dad that she'd lost a shoe nor would she ease my conscience for my bad attitude.

Granted, I should have been gentler in the way I handled it. That's one of the things for which I know I am forgiven. But it too was a valuable lesson.

We are all free to make decisions whatever way we wish, but for each decision there will be consequences. Did I ever tell her I was sorry for my behavior? Yes, many years later.

Whether it is a choice of drug or alcohol usage, sexual practices or something as minor as disciplining a child (can a mistake in disciplining a child be called minor?), we make our choices, but we must remember each one will have its own consequences which will affect our lives and those of the people we love.

Please, God, help us to make wise choices.

A FAREWELL REMEMBERED

Howard had always been a strong man, able to repair anything or make anything he wished. I recall when we met, he was able to hunker down to take an eighty-five horsepower Ford engine out of the car in his arms, pick it up and carry it to a bench several feet away. He wouldn't even break a sweat. He wasn't some muscular athlete with bulging biceps. He was five foot eight inches and weighed maybe one hundred fifty pounds at the most.

Pushups were a cinch for him, so he did one-arm pushups and would continue until I lost count of them. When people were properly impressed, he would bend over backwards and put his hands flat on the floor. He was able to do these exercises due to the training he received in the military in WW II.

He was never wounded in combat, but he had other *battle scars*—bad dreams, and for nearly ten years after we were married, he had a groove in his shoulder where one of his weapons, a .30 caliber air-cooled machine gun, had rested. That groove eventually disappeared, but the permanent injury was to his hearing.

Forty years after his discharge, the Veterans Administration determined that he was totally deaf in his left ear and had less than twenty percent hearing in the right ear. They provided him with hearing aids of progressively greater strength in an attempt to help him communicate with the world.

His deafness wasn't what people usually think of, which is total silence or a total lack of sound. His deafness consisted of strange noises and muffled

153

sounds. The sound of people talking and laughing made him so uncomfortable that he would leave the situation. Crying babies caused him pain; imagine someone blowing a shrill whistle in your ear! There was only a certain range of voices he was able to discern. Thankfully, mine was one of them. I always went to appointments with him back then because I could make him understand what others said.

I told people, "You don't have to shout at him. Speak slowly, enunciate clearly, and use as few words as possible."

We were together for fifty-seven years when he reached the point where his strength began to fail. Gradually, his body energies were drained until he was so frail he was unable to stand up without assistance.

The last few weeks were heartbreaking to watch. I was grateful to be physically able to provide the care and assistance he needed. While his strength waned, his deep and abiding faith in his Lord grew, and he was prepared to take that step into eternity without fear or apprehension.

He was in the hospital in kidney failure. The doctor said he would go into a coma and just slip away. We were almost looking forward to a coma so he would be free of the pain associated with his other problems. The hospital staff understood why I had to be with him so much. Visiting hours were waved for me and I am so grateful for that.

The last few days, his hearing aids began to malfunction. They became a source of aggravation to both of us. Again, a coma would have been a relief. That last day, I gave up on them and put them away. I was able to communicate that to him, and he understood. He was weak, but alert.

A few hours later, one of our daughters came in to tell him that she'd taken his cat to her house. He smiled weakly and squeezed her hand. He'd heard! As minutes passed, we were able to speak to him in whispers and he heard! I had raised the head of the bed so it was easier for him to breathe and to relieve the rattle in his throat.

He kept looking in the corner of the ceiling, as if he were seeing something that captivated his attention. Somehow, we knew his time was short. As he kept looking up, I told him that when the angels came for him, to go with them. I would be alright because he had taught me what I needed to know to care for myself. He should go ahead, and in time I would be following him.

My daughter began to quietly sing a chorus sun in many churches.

There's a sweet, sweet spirit in this place,
And I know that it's the Spirit of the Lord.
There are sweet expressions on each face,
And I know they feel the presence of the Lord.

Chorus:
Sweet Holy Spirit, sweet heavenly dove,
Stay right here with us,
Filling us with Your love
And for these blessings
We will lift our hearts in praise
Without a doubt we'll know

That we have been revived
When we shall leave this place.[1]

What words can describe the emotions that we felt? Love? Joy? Grief? The word bittersweet comes to mind. Tears were generously flowing, while a beautiful peace filled the room.

All this time, his eyes were focused on that corner. Then he made a motion with his arms, which my daughter described as if he were opening a curtain. He lifted his head and shoulders from the pillows, extending his arms up to reach out for something, and then suddenly he was gone.

Every wrinkle in his face disappeared, and his skin glowed. I never wished to have him back, but I wept for myself. My other half had been torn away, and it was painful. That day was more than five years ago on Feb 27, 2004.

Until a few days ago, every time I heard that song, my mind went back to that hospital room, and I would weep. On a recent Sunday, as the music started for that chorus, I mentally tried to brace myself. Thank God, this time something different happened.

As the music and voices were raised, it was as if the Lord reached deep inside me, and with His healing balm, He took away the awful ache of loneliness. He impressed on me that every time I hear that song again,

---

[1]*Sweet, Sweet Spirit*, by Doris Akers; © Copyright 1962. Renewed 1990 by Manna Music, Inc., 35255 Brooten Road, Pacific City, OR 97135. All Rights Reserved. Used by Permission. (ASCAP)

I would only remember the grace and love which was showered on me that day.

I will always remember those blessings, as well as the many promises made to those who believe and accept Christ as Savior.

- John 11:25-26—He gives us the promise of eternal life.
- 1 Corinthians 15:51-55—We are promised we have a new body with no aches or pains.
- 1 Thessalonians 4:14-18—We are promised that we will be reunited with our loved ones who have gone before.
- Revelations 21:2-7—We are promised that we will be with Him for all eternity.

What more could we ask?

(Scriptures quoted from the NKJV)

TIME—WHAT IS IT?

Joshua 10:13-14 says, "The sun stopped in the midst of heaven, and did not hasten to go down for about a whole day. There has been no day like it before or after it, that the Lord heeded the voice of a man." (NKJV)

Time. One definition I've heard for time is "a period between two eternities." Have you ever wished time could stand still?

As I write this, it is the second anniversary of my husband's death on February 27, 2004. Has it only been seven hundred thirty days since he slipped the surly bonds of this ailing, pain-wracked body and went to be with his God?

Two years—a period of time between two eternities. Some wise man once said that time and everything is relative. Perhaps he was right.

We were together over fifty-seven years. Sometimes, while looking back it seems as if we'd been together all of my life. Other times, it was as if those years were compressed into months or even mere weeks.

In the years since, my life has been totally upset and turned around. There I was, seventy-two years old, and for the first time in my life I was going to live alone.

That next fall, two ladies named Frances and Jeanne (hurricanes for non-Floridians) destroyed my home barely six months after Howard's death.

For a while, I lived in what I laughingly called my "sardine can," a small travel trailer courtesy of

F.E.M.A., but I called it home. Now looking back at those eleven months, they seemed to be unending time.

I was finally able to move into my new home in the late summer of 2005. I felt that now I would be able to start my new life. It was too easy to forget that we are never promised tomorrow. Humans plan and God laughs. Don't get too comfortable. What's next?

Next was a lady named Wilma. She didn't do too much harm to me, but she did remind me life is short at its best so savor each moment.

I look back on my life in awe, and realize how much I've been blessed. I've had the love of a good and faithful man, a family, children, thirteen grandchildren, and now fourteen great-grandchildren. Number fourteen great-grandchild arrived in September of 2008. I had a sister and I've been blessed with friends.

When we moved to Florida, we found a home, a church family, and friends who replaced those who've gone on before us. These past days, weeks, and months have been a wonderful learning experience for me.

Each day I've had to realize again how very weak I am. **But God**! He has been with me, leading, strengthening and encouraging me.

Some of those days have seemed devastating, but in those dark times, I've learned how vital it is for me to know that God loves me. In the best and worst of those times, He has been with me.

But God has become one of my favorite phrases in the Bible. How often we read of folks getting into trouble, straying from the covenants they have made with the Creator, and at the last minute during a moment of crisis, He steps in and we read, **"But God"** as He moves in His sovereign manner.

If I go to the beach and try to pick up just one grain of sand, I am reminded how very small I am in the grand scheme of things. One grain of sand on a beach, but I know that God knows me and even knows how many hairs are on my head.

Time and grains of sand on a beach are reminders that my lifetime is but a period—.— a small dot between two eternities.

MOTHER'S FURNITURE-MOVING FRIEND

I don't remember her name, but she was a good friend of my mother's. When I was about nine years old, this event occurred on a weekend about a year after my daddy was killed in an accident.

Mother said she just needed to get out of town for a day or two, so she packed the few clothes we might need, loaded my sister and me into her 1941 Plymouth Business Coupe, and away we went. I don't recall for certain, but somewhere in the back of my brain I think we went to Coldwater, Michigan.

Strange, the whole trip has been lost in my memory. I recall a couple of little boys and the friend's house. Right off of the living room was a tall staircase which led to two or three bedrooms and a bathroom.

What is clear in my mind is the image of that little woman, trying to move a huge chair. Well, it seemed huge to me, as I was quite small for my age. It was what they call a *club chair*, big, overstuffed, and heavy.

She told my mother she wanted to get it out of the living room because she didn't like the color. As she started to slide it toward the stairs, mother stepped in to help her.

"No," she said. "I can get it. Just stay out of my way."

Mother tried to argue with her, but the friend remained adamant and refused any help. So Mother just stood aside and said, "Then do it yourself."

She moved that chair around until it faced the stairwell, and then suddenly, she sat down on it. I watched as she reached around with her arms until she was holding the back of the chair. She took several deep breaths and leaned forward until I thought she would fall over on her nose. As she stood up, the chair rose, balanced on her back. After a few more deep breaths, she walked up the stairs, chair and all, without stopping until she reached the room she was headed for. Arriving there, she leaned forward and slowly sat down and the chair was in place.

I was awestruck. I had heard about really strong men, but never about a woman who could do anything like that. Wow!

"See, I told you I could do it," she crowed.

Mother just uttered something, but I was speechless.

I think about her now and ponder how much we can be like that woman. Situations arise in lives which appear to be unconquerable. We just flex our muscles, bend into the job and do it. Perhaps we may even injure ourselves.

Why is it that we don't ask for help when there is someone standing there who is ready and willing to help lift the load? Ecclesiastes 4:9 says, "Two are better than one; because they have a good reward for their labor." (NKJV)

The Lord is always there, standing by, ready to help us lift our spiritual loads if we only ask Him; and He will give us a good reward for asking for His help.

CHILDREN'S CHILDREN

When we were having babies and raising kids, the concept of one day having grandchildren was not in the forefront of my mind. Time whizzed by, and on March 5th, 1967, I found myself sitting in the waiting room of our local OB unit. I'd had a problem the past few months of accepting the fact that I would be a grandma. As I watched my daughter's body expand and change, I began to accept the reality.

A gray-haired LPN who worked in the nursery of the unit entered. As she passed me, she stopped. "What are you doing here?" she asked me.

I told her I was waiting to hear the cry of my first grandchild.

"No way," she gasped. "It hasn't been that long since I brought your first baby to you. Stay there; I'll be right back," She turned and headed to the delivery room. As she opened the door I heard a plaintive cry, which soon became a healthy howl.

"He's here," she reported. A few minutes later she returned with all the vital statistics.

Watching him grow from an infant to a toddler was such fun. I remember him trying to be like his granddad, who had given the lad a miniature corncob pipe like his. The little guy would walk around with the pipe in his mouth and hold it in his hand as he spoke.

Soon it was time for him to go to school. I found it a joy to go with him to the pre-school clinic and observe as he was given fluoride treatments. He smiled all the time.

A little sister joined him along the way. Again, I have so many memories which bring a smile to my face. I was thankful that I was able to make a costume for her for a school party, *Raggedy Anne*, complete with a string-mop wig.

More years passed, and another daughter's baby boy was born. I enjoyed carrying him around because he looked like a little old man. A form of Albinism caused his hair and eyebrows to be snow-white. A special memory of him occurred when he was bout four. It was October, and the Michigan weather had changed the leaves to brilliant reds, golds, and oranges.

I had been busy raking the leaves, getting them to the side of the road to be burned, and piling them quite high. Without warning, I picked him up and threw him into the pile, and then jumped in after him. When we tired of the game, we discovered the leaves were all over the yard again. I didn't mind doing the job over. The joy of that memory made me forget my aching back.

More little girls and boys arrived until the total reached thirteen. For a variety of reasons, I wasn't able to have fun with many of them. Families moved to other states, and other things made it difficult to get to know them.

Another mental picture I have is one of the little girls, about age two, wearing bib-top overalls, helping her daddy work on the brakes of his car. This dainty, little thing was "helping him" by carrying his tools around the garage while getting her hands covered with grease.

I recall the time my son's daughter wanted a new bike—a big two-wheeler. Money was tight for them, but I had a nice bike which I seldom used. I worked a deal with the girl; if she would mow my grass for two weeks, then she would earn the bike for her own. The deal was done, and it gave me such joy to look out my window and see her vigorously walking behind the mower. The joy grew as I watched her dad lift the bike into his truck, and I saw her smile as they drove away.

My last two granddaughters lived over three hundred miles away, but we were blessed in that we could visit them, and they us.

On one visit, for some unknown reason, my husband bought several rubber band powered balsa wood airplanes. It didn't take him long to show them how to fly those planes, and all was well until they became stuck high in a pine tree or made crash landings.

Now the grandchildren are grown and have families of their own. He has blessed me with fourteen great-grandchildren. They all live far away from me, but I still love each one and keep them all in my prayers.

As I think about all of those precious ones, I can only think of Proverbs 17:6, which says, "Children's children are the crown of an old man." (NKJV) Someplace else it says that those children are the reward for gray hair.

I know that surely the same reward applies equally to old women. I wear my crown of my children's children proudly and thank God for each of them.

THE OTHER ROOM

Our grandparents found a small, very old, one-bedroom house, probably built back in the 1800's. The elderly couple, who owned it wanted to spend winter and spring in Florida and thought our grandparents, in their seventies at the time, would be the ideal renters. The owners wouldn't have to worry about their house being torn up or destroyed by partying young people.

So our grandparents moved in. It was the first time in their lives they had hot, running water.

Winter and spring passed quickly. As the summer arrived, Grandmother's health began to fail rapidly. The doctor told the family she was having mini strokes, nothing terribly unusual, but the drastic change in her behavior frightened her husband.

As these spells would come on her, she behaved erratically and talked unlike herself. The sad thing about them was that after the spells passed, she remembered the strange things she said and did. That upset her very much. She had always been so strong and solid, and the family always looked to her for its strength.

In late July her brother and his wife drove up from Ohio to visit them for a few days. When they arrived, grandmother enjoyed showing then around from room to room in the little house. In one corner of the kitchen, there was a small, built-in cupboard; some called it a hutch. The homeowners' fancy dishes were still displayed on the shelves.

As she stood, leaning on the table, she pointed with her cane at the cabinet and said, "In there is the loveliest room in the house, but we aren't allowed to go in there; it isn't ready yet."

When any visitors came, she gave them the same tour and said the same thing about that corner cabinet. People would look at each other, roll their eyes, and not say anything about it. One day her daughter dropped in and was given the tour, and told the same thing.

"Mama, stop saying that! There isn't another room in there. It's just a cabinet!"

I happened to be standing right beside Grandmother when those words were spoken. She turned to me and said, "She can't see it, can she? She just doesn't understand what that room is, does she?

I agreed she didn't understand, wondering to myself whether I did. Was Grandmother seeing a room which wasn't visible to us? A room which was an entry into heaven?

John 14:2-3 in THE MESSAGE says this: "There is plenty of room in my Father's home. If that weren't so, would I have told you that I'm on my way to get a room ready for you? And if I'm on my way to get your room ready, I'll come back and get you so you can live where I live."

Less than one month later, Grandmother went home to be with the Lord, very quietly and with a clear mind. I was privileged to be with her at that time. I often wondered; did she go into that room or was there one even nicer waiting for her?

Since that time I have committed my life to the Lord. I am now certain beyond any doubt that the lovely room was there, and it is as beautiful as she had thought.

HAIL TO THE VICTORS

In southeastern Michigan, it was almost a required part of learning that we knew the words and music to the University of Michigan Fight Song. "Hail to the Victors valiant, Hail to the conquering heroes. Hail, hail to Michigan. . ." Even when I wasn't a football fan, I really liked that song.

While football wasn't my cup of tea, I always had a "hero complex." Those were the days of World War II when a large number of our local boys were in the armed forces. Our school assigned each student the name of a local boy who was in the service. The intent was to encourage the young men in the military. We were to write to "our soldier," and report back to the class when we received any answer.

Most of the kids only wrote once or twice and then got bored with the idea of it, but I maintained correspondence with my soldier all through the war. My mother told me that he had worked with my daddy, and all of the fellows called him Whitey because of his light blond hair. Every time I got a letter from him, I proudly gave my class the full report. He sent me photographs of himself and his new bride when he married her in California before he was sent overseas. I kept writing to him even when I didn't know where he was. I learned later that he had been in Italy, France, and Germany.

One day in the spring of 1945 when I was thirteen years old, my mother phoned me from her work and told me to get cleaned up, as there was somebody she wanted me to meet. She knew me well enough to know I would need to be cleaned up because

I was very much in my tomboy phase. I hurried to get ready and Mom soon came to get me. I hoped into the car and we headed to town.

When we drove up to a house, I saw a handsome soldier sitting on the porch; it was my Whitey! What a marvelous surprise! He had stopped home just long enough to spend a little time with his parents.

The war in Europe was over, and his unit was given leave prior to being sent to the Pacific area. I asked him why he didn't have any hair because his head had been shaved. He told me that when they were loaded into the troop transport, they all decided that as long as they weren't going home they might as well shave their heads. After they had all done it, their officers told them that orders had been changed and they were going home after all.

We had a wonderful visit together before he had to get ready to travel to California, where his wife was waiting for him. For years after that, he and his wife would exchange Christmas cards with me—even after I was married. Somehow, as years passed, we lost touch with each other, as so often happens.

Sometime in the mid-1960's my husband and I attended the funeral of one of our friend's dads. At the luncheon after the service, I kept noticing this man across the room. He looked strangely familiar, but I had never known any of the rest of that family.

I asked my friend who he was. She didn't know his real name; all she knew was that everyone called him Whitey. It was him! Again, we had a joyful reunion. In my mind, he was still "my soldier," and to him I was still his little friend.

In the years since then, I have watched dear friends, schoolmates of my sons' and even my grandsons' leave home and family to serve our nation. Too often their return home was the occasion for tears at a military funeral or that one of them had lost a leg or another limb.

But there were also the joyful returns. In 1991, my oldest grandson was serving aboard the aircraft carrier *USS America* when that battle group was deployed to the Gulf during the *Desert Storm* conflict.

While looking through old copies of a newsletter I had put together back then, I ran across a story I had written about that homecoming. That triggered many memories, as well as deep emotions, which were easily forgotten. Let me share a bit of it with you.

I had the privilege to be present at the homecoming of that ship, as she returned to her home port in Norfolk, Virginia. If there were a way to put emotions on paper to share with you the joy and excitement that was felt by all present, it would take more paper and talent than I have.

The huge aircraft carrier was pushed to her spot on the pier by the little tugboats; black smoke was belching from their stacks. On the pier, people 25,000 strong, were all yelling and screaming at the top of their lungs. The Navy band had been playing a march until the ship's P.A. system began blaring the song *Coming to America*. The crew was lined up all around the perimeter of the flight deck, standing at attention until all lines were made fast.

No matter where one would look, flags were flying, yellow ribbons were everywhere and banners of all sorts were waving. People were holding up handmade signs with the name of the particular sailor they were waiting for. If it wasn't possible to see the activity from a spot by the fence, people were climbing on whatever was available to get a better view. I was grateful that we had driven our big station wagon, and by standing on the tailgate, I could see over the tops of people's heads.

In the midst of all this, the Navy's *Blue Angels*, the precision flying team of jets, did a flyover. The roar of their engines was nearly drowned out by the cheers and screams of the people as they passed overhead.

That day, laughing, crying, even hugging strangers, were all perfectly acceptable behavior as the men came down the gangplank to find the ones they loved.

In the crew of over three thousand and their families, it was a miracle to be able to find each other.

I was separated in the crowd and couldn't find my grandson or the rest of our family. As I was trying to find them, my eye caught sight of one very young sailor who had no one to greet him. When I asked if he had family present, he answered, "No, Ma'am, my family couldn't come. My granny was too sick to leave her."

After I asked if I could be his "granny" for the day, his eyes filled with tears and he nodded. We embraced and I thanked God for his safe return and welcomed him home."

That day, *Hail to the Victors* would definitely have been appropriate, for these men were literally being given a hero's welcome.

One day, there will be another great return of a "conquering hero" when people all over the world will be called to pay homage to Him. Even in a crowd that large, there won't be any problem seeing Him. He will be looking for each one of us.

That day will be the grandest welcome mission ever held. Romans 14:11 (NKJV) puts it this way; "Every knee shall bow to Me, and every tongue shall confess to God."

Are you looking forward to that day with joy or dread? He can either be your Redeemer and Savior or your worst nightmare. You make the choice.

SEED BAG DRESSES

One of the nicest things my husband gave me was an electric sewing machine. For several years after we were married, I had used an old-fashioned treadle sewing machine. As I write those words, I cannot help but wonder how many readers will even know what a treadle sewing machine was. Perhaps the best way to describe it is to say it had a foot-operated device. The treadle was similar to a doublewide accelerator on a car. When you rocked your feet back and forth, it caused the sewing part of the machine to work.

This was the device I used to hem six or seven dozen diapers (there weren't disposables ones in those days). I made the diapers out of white flannel along with the *belly bands*. These consisted of several layers of bands of flannel, which were wrapped around the navel to keep the cord clean and dry. It was not unusual to have to replace a band with each diaper change, especially for baby boys. Receiving blankets in which we swaddled the baby were made out of soft flannel about forty-two inches square. That type of sewing didn't require much skill, just the ability to sew a straight line.

As the girl babies grew, making pretty dresses presented more of a challenge. Ruffles, frills, puffed sleeves, buttonholes and such, required more skill, but they were a real joy to work on.

When our first girl was nearing three years old, I couldn't wait until I could make those pretty things for her. That's when I received the electric sewer. It had attachments, which enabled me to make buttonholes, gather and ruche the material into fancy designs, and I could sew on hem binding so that it didn't show.

I was able to gather several inches of material, put it on a tiny cuff, and then set it all into the sleeve line. It made me want to burst with pride in my workmanship. Those dresses were so cute. I just loved to wash and even iron them. I would lay the sleeve flat and iron it into a circle. After they were starched, they stood up when the dress was worn. I remember standing and admiring my handiwork when they were all ironed and hanging together.

Our second baby was a boy, and there weren't a lot of fancy things he needed. His items just had to be serviceable and double-kneed, that is, I needed to sew a second layer of fabric onto the knees to reinforce them.

Another little girl came, and I was really proud of the skills I had developed. There was just one problem—now the yard goods which I had been buying went up in price. That, plus the fact of having three children meant each dollar had to go farther. Then I made a discovery.

I found a store which sold seeds and supplies to farmers and gardeners. Seeds, in bulk, were packed in twenty-five pound bags. Those bags were made of fairly sturdy, but nice, material, printed with flowers, birds, and that sort of thing. I could buy the bags for twenty-five cents apiece, or six for a dollar. All I had to do was to sort through the pile until I found the prints I wanted, trying not to sneeze too many times. After they were laundered and ironed, I could get one dress or two blouses out of one bag. Such a deal!

As the girls grew, it took a second bag for a dress, but it still was a bargain. I don't recall when I stopped using the seed bags. My first impulse is to say it was about the time the oldest girl became fashion conscious, but I don't think that's right. I think it was because the store closed due to lack of business.

I really enjoyed all the comments I received from friends and grandparents as they oohed and aahed about how nice the girls looked in their dresses. Our friends would ask me to make things for their little girls too.

Then I remembered "do not be proud, for the Lord has spoken" in Jeremiah 13:15 (NKJV). That helped me to focus on the blessings the Lord bestowed on us. It wasn't my skill, but His leading me through the seed bags.

WILL YOU TAKE A CHECK?

When we were first married, we operated on a *cash only* basis. It wasn't until we experienced having paid a bill in cash, mislaying the receipt, and having to pay it the second time that we decided to open a checking account.

My husband wasn't entirely supportive of the idea. He'd heard many stories from his grandparents about people losing their money when the banks closed during the depression years.

We went to the bank on a payday, opened the account, and deposited the cash, saving a few dollars for daily expenses. Thus began the adventure of writing checks and reconciling the account each month.

The first several months went well, and I began to feel smug and sure of myself as a check-writer. Then I discovered my first mistake in math and the disaster it caused. Well, it wasn't exactly a disaster, but it certainly felt like it at the time.

Just to state that I was overdrawn by eighteen dollars doesn't sound like a lot of money. When you take into consideration the fact that Howard's weekly paycheck was around thirty-five dollars, it resonates much larger.

Fortunately, he had squirreled away a few dollars, as had I. We were able to cover the shortage with nothing more than terribly wounded pride.

As the years passed we exercised more caution. We settled down and the program worked well for us. We began to get smug again. If a bill was due on Saturday and we knew Howard would be paid on Friday, I'd mail the check early. My thought was that by the time the check got back to the bank, the money would be there. That worked well for a period of time.

Then came the day we didn't make it to the bank on time. The check was marked "return for insufficient funds" (NSF) in red letters by the bank, and they sent it back to the power company. It wasn't long before we got a phone call from the power company. They weren't happy.

The next sad experience was the way we learned about NSF fees. Our bank charged us a fee to cover the expense of returning the check to the power company. The power company charged a fee for dealing with their bank.

We learned what it meant for a check to bounce. Boing, boing, boing! Each bounce incurred a fee, and suddenly we were in a hole, getting deeper by the hour, or so it seemed.

We discovered we weren't the only people who made that sort of mistake. That didn't help the embarrassment we felt when we walked into the bank. We were sure everyone in there knew how we had fouled up. When we went into the power company, I think the people smirked behind our backs, laughing at the two who couldn't balance a checkbook.

We worked through that situation too and came out of it wiser and more attentive to the importance of correct math. It impacts us even more when we compare writing a check in our name and asking God for something in the name of His Son, Jesus. He has given us authority to ask whatever we will in the name of Jesus, and He will grant it. We don't have to worry about insufficient funds. Our account might be overdrawn, but His never is. He owns the cattle on a thousand hills; all the gold and the silver in the world were created by Him.

Would you take His check?

FAITH IN OUR PARENTS

In the late 1970's, we left our big house in the country with four bedrooms, the one-acre lawn, and the three-and-a-half-car garage to move into a small house in town. Financial reverses made the move necessary, and in all honesty, the move was not exactly a happy one.

We were used to the privacy and quiet of the country, and we had had many neighbors there with lots of children for ours to play with and things to entertain them there, but the houses weren't really close. By the time we were ready to sell the large home, our older children were grown, so we didn't really need all of the bedrooms.

The house in town had two bedrooms upstairs. Downstairs there was a living room, dining room, kitchen, another bedroom, and one small room facing the south, which was perfect for my sewing room. Oh yes, the house had one-an-a-half bathrooms too.

The biggest drawback for my husband was the fact that there was no garage.

For me, the worst thing was that the neighbor's house on one side was only about fifteen feet from ours. That neighbor was a single mother of two small boys. They were always running in and out of the house, slamming the doors as they went. I made a point to keep the windows on that side of the house closed and the curtains drawn.

We soon learned that she was training those boys to become gentlemen—some day. They used the words *please*, *thank you*, *ma'am*, and *sir*. That was a

185

pleasant surprised, but they were still healthy boys of the ages of six and seven, noisy and energetic.

Another boy lived across the street, the son of two working parents. He could learn much from Betty's boys. The event which sticks in my mind happened one day when the neighbor boy across the street was home alone. All of the children were playing a very noisy game. Something happened and I heard the *home-alone boy* scream. Rushing to the front door to see what had happened, I could see him. Blood dripped from his hand.

The oldest *next door boy* pulled his kerchief from his pocket, wrapped it around the hand, and said to him, "Come to my house. My mom can fix anything."

Three boys dashed through the door to Betty's house, letting it bang three times behind each of them.

As I went back to whatever project I was working on at the time, I couldn't help but think about what the boy had said.

My mom can fix anything.

He had absolute faith in his mother. This boy had no question of whether it may have been too serious for her, or the possibility she wouldn't want to help someone else's child. Just simply, his mom could fix anything.

How many times in life have we had the opportunity to rush to the aid of someone who was hurting, wrap a temporary bandage around the wound, and say, "Come to my God, my Father; He can fix anything."

If you have failed as often as I have, let us together ask our Father to forgive us; to help us grow

186

our faith and confidence; to become bold for His name's sake.

DO YOU LISTEN TO YOUR WIFE?

We always enjoyed camping, whether in tents, campers, travel trailers, or whatever. We loved going into the woods and savoring the sounds and fragrances of the forest. November in Michigan is dear season, and the woods would be full of people like us who wanted to get away from it all.

One year, another couple joined us for a mini-hunting trip. This was to be a two-day adventure. We packed our rifles, food, supplies, camping gear, and things we were sure we'd need. When I proposed a change of clothing, the men pooh-poohed the idea.

"We're only going to be gone two days. Why do we need a change of clothes?"

Do I have to tell you that my friend and I took a change of clothes, despite our husbands' protests?

We left late on a Friday evening, planning to arrive at our favorite spot in plenty of time to get our tent set up and get in a good nap before the men would head out into the woods before daylight.

At dawn they went out for an hour or so. Then they came back in to have breakfast. Nothing smells quite as good as coffee brewing and bacon frying on a brisk morning in the forest. After about an hour they headed out again.

We suggested that it might rain before they came back, so perhaps they should stay near the camp. Again, what would we know?

Around noon, my friend and I fixed a good, warm meal, which we ate quickly, being sure to save

189

some for the men to eat whenever they came back. She and I played cards and talked and talked. We enjoyed being away from our usual routine. The afternoon passed, and it began to rain. As the hours went by, we became concerned because the men were still not back. It gets dark early in Michigan in November, and we considered the possibility that they might have gotten lost in the woods, something nobody wants to ever happen.

To signal lost hunters, it is well-known that those in camp fire three shots, which would enable them to locate the right direction to head for the camp. All around us in several directions we could hear three shots being fired. How on earth would our men know which ones were from our camp?

We decided to blow the car horn three times. We did this every few minutes for nearly an hour. Finally, we saw two pitiful-looking men walking up the road.

They told the story of "the biggest buck we ever saw." They had taken a shot, hit it, and the deer ran off into the forest. Hunters don't leave a wounded animal, so they began to track it.

The buck headed deeper and deeper into the swamp until the mighty hunters lost its trail. There they were in the swamp; it was pouring rain, getting dark, and they were lost.

They heard the horn and followed it back to the camp when they walked out of the woods onto the road.

Which brings us to the moral of the story. Why would we need a change of clothes? They were dripping wet and soaked to the skin. In fact, they were so wet that even the bills on their caps drooped. They sat shivering in the tent, sitting almost on top of the stove in an attempt to get warm as they swallowed cup after cup of coffee until they'd emptied the third pot.

I had brought along an extra pair of slacks and a sweater, which would fit my friend's husband, but my husband was out of luck. After they peeled off the wet clothes, Howard had to settle for wrapping up in a blanket while we girls took all of the wet things to find a Laundromat where we could use the clothes dryer. The nearest town happened to be fifteen miles away.

Proverbs 31 says that a good wife is more precious than gems, all the days of her life—especially if she doesn't say, "I told you so!"

I BEG YOUR PARDON

I always felt deep in my heart that God has a sense of humor. He made me, didn't He? My early image of Him was of a great, white-haired, bearded creature sitting behind a big bench. He was a judge, waiting for me to get out of line so he could knock me down.

Of course, after I committed my life to Him, that image has totally changed. He became a loving Father. I thank Him for the earthly father He gave me, even though he died when I was very young. My mental picture of my daddy is of the times he would pick me up and carry me around on his shoulders. It was easy for me to think of God as a loving, merciful Father. I know not everyone was blessed to have that kind of Daddy.

In those early months after I found Him, I was much like many baby Christians; I had made the decision for Him, and assumed that now life was going to be peachy keen. Wrong!

Having had three teen-agers, and surviving them, I thought that nothing new could possibly happen. Wrong! There are still two left at home.

One day I was extremely upset over something one of them had done, and I dissolved into tears, having a first class pity-party. I wept and literally collapsed to the floor, crying.

"Oh God, why did this happen? Why do I have to suffer like this? And on and on, ad nausea. I sat there on the floor, emoting to the highest degree. Somewhere in the house I heard a radio. A disc jockey was playing a very popular song.

"I beg your pardon; I never promised you a rose garden."[2]

I didn't know God used DJs too to get His point across to us. I learned that day He does have a sense of humor. I could almost hear Him laughing with me.

LOOK BEFORE YOU GRAB

Even when our children were small, we enjoyed camping. Most of our early camping days were done in tents. We had every type of equipment we could think of to make our *roughing it* more comfortable. If Coleman made it, we had it.

I really appreciated our small table with four seats, which folded up to be smaller than a suitcase. We used it as a kitchen counter most of the time, and rarely used it as a table because the parks always had a large picnic table at each site for use at meal times, along with a fire-pit. Some even had electrical outlets.

On one of our childless trips we decided to go to the nearby town to have breakfast, and then take a driving tour of the area. I'd taken a shower earlier that morning in the community bathhouse. Back at our tent we sat at that little table, discussing the day ahead. I was doing what I could to make myself beautiful by trying to make my hair presentable. This was something I never had much luck with.

As we discussed the various points of interest, I came to the realization I couldn't do any better. I reached across the table for the can of hairspray. After applying it, the thought came to me that it smelled strange. Meantime, my husband was laughing himself silly. I had missed the joke.

When he was able to control himself, he said drolly, "You shouldn't have any trouble with the mosquitoes today. "

Then I realized the reason it smelled strange wasn't from hairspray; it was bug repellent.

195

I paraphrased Ecclesiastes Chapter 2:1 to him in this way, "I'm telling you from my heart. Go on now! Enjoy yourself, I'll see who laughs last. . . behold all is vanity! You don't have to rub it in."

Right then our plan for the day changed. We did have breakfast, but the first stop was to find a beauty shop where I could have my hair washed and set. I was not about to spend the entire day smelling like a bug bomb!

As foolish as I felt that morning, even after several years, Howard would tease me. "Are you sure you grabbed the right can?" And we'd laugh together.

That wasn't the only time we had a laugh over problems with my hair. One such occasion happened as I was getting ready for church. I had slept in curlers the night before. The few rollers in front had fallen out, so I put them back in place and proceeded to get the children fed and ready to go.

In the rush, I forgot about those curlers and went merrily on my way. In the middle of the service, I inadvertently put my hand to my forehead, and there they were, as nice as you please. I pretended not to notice them until we were in the car. Then I angrily demanded to know why he hadn't told me they were there.

"I thought you wanted them there."

The moral of this story is to be certain of what you are doing before you do it! Remember, all is vanity.

LESSONS FROM THE SHRUBBERY

As the children grew, I developed an interest in yard work; not mowing the grass, but in making the yard look nice. I'd plant annuals around the trees, along the edge of the driveway, and everywhere I could see them. On one side of the house, we had a few shrubs growing. They were pretty, but they weren't close enough to screen the view of our neighbor's collection of cars.

Trying to recall what Granddad had told me about such things, I decided to see if I could make the shrubs fill in that gap. I used cuttings from the shrubs to try to get a root started, but with no luck.

I thought of a different way to attempt this project, so I pulled down one of the longer branches from two shrubs, which were about twenty-four inches apart. I dug a shallow hole and buried one end of each branch. The "parent" bushes were so strong they kept pulling the branches out of the ground. Not to be easily discouraged, I found a good size rock and placed it on top of my future shrub. Perhaps not terribly clever, but it worked.

After a few months my little project took root. When I lifted the rock, my baby shrub stayed in the ground. Soon after, I took my loping shears and cut the baby plants away from the parents. They needed to be separated from each other in order for all of them to continue to grow strong.

When I admired my handiwork, the thought came to mind that perhaps those shrubs could be compared to two sets of parents. The "project" could be compared to a young man and a young woman who are starting their new lives as man and wife.

The Bible tells us that a man should cleave to his wife and forsake all others. It is important for each set of parents to be there to help the young people if they need it and if they ask for it. Sometimes it might be necessary to put something heavy or stressful on them to keep the new roots growing and to protect them from the power of the rains and storms which threaten to uproot them.

There must come a time when the new marriage must stand alone. One of them, or perhaps both, may have to speak plainly to their parents. It will become necessary for the new shrub to establish boundaries. This must be done in love and with respect, but it must be done in order to have a healthy, new plant, able to grow and stand on its own.

Otherwise, how could they stay together and become as one?

THE BROKEN DOLL BABY

When she was about four or five years old, one of my granddaughters had a special doll. Her baby had moveable legs and arms. The shoulders, elbows, hips, and knees were all jointed; a ball-and-socket joint was made of some type of moldable material.

That doll baby went everywhere she went. One day they were at our house. The children had been playing outdoors when suddenly the front door burst open. She stormed into the house, weeping and wailing, and ran straight to her daddy.

After he calmed her down, he asked her what happened to make her feel so bad.

She started crying again, and through the sobs, she said, "She's broke and she's going to die!" Then she showed him the doll and the arm, which had come out of its socket.

He scooped her up into his lap. "Let me see what I can do for her," he gently said.

After thinking about it awhile, he decided to put a drop or two of oil on the ball and socket, and one good turn should make the baby as good as new. He let the child slip easily from his lap and stood to go to his dad's workshop.

"Don't take her away from me!" she screamed again, and continued sobbing. He tried to explain to her that he was only going to get a tool to fix her, and that he'd be right back. This didn't stop her crying or make her understand his plan.

Instead, she seized the doll and ran off to hide outdoors in the yard, slamming the door behind her.

"I know I can fix it good as new, be she won't let go of it." Her daddy looked at me, frustrated, with tears in his eyes. "She won't give it to me and trust me to make it right."

I couldn't help but think how much more does our heavenly Father hurt when we won't entrust our pain and our brokenness to Him. Just as her daddy was prepared to mend the broken doll, our Daddy God is always ready, willing, and able to mend any problem we take to Him. But we must be prepared to totally surrender it to Him. We must trust Him to do what is best for us.

CONSIDER THE TURTLE

In the winter of 1982, our youngest daughter had married, and for the first time in nearly thirty-five years, our home was childless. It was now just my husband and me and a cat and a dog. How should we act?

Howard was still working, and I kept busy volunteering. I had often thought how nice it would be if we could travel—not around the world, but to someplace different where we didn't have to drive, but could be chauffeured and waited on.

I investigated the bus tours I'd seen advertised in the papers. They would last four or five days and visit some beautiful spots in Michigan, as well as other states. The prices were not unreasonable.

Howard said that if I wanted to do that, it would be okay with him; he'd like to go along too. Every place I called gave me the big pitch about how many nights we'd be in a four star hotel, how fabulous the meals would be, and the sights we'd see. And, of course, we would always be greeted at our hotels with champagne and cocktails.

Neither of us were drinkers, especially not of champagne. When I inquired if there would be a break in the cost if we didn't take that option, their response was always the same; *Use it or lose it.* I've always been pretty stingy, and the idea of paying for something I wouldn't use rubbed me the wrong way. After talking with several different agencies, I discovered they all operated the same way.

One evening I reported my findings to Howard. I figured I might as well forget about the idea.

He looked at me seriously and said, "If you don' like the way they're operated, why don't you do it your way? You're a Christian; pray about it."

When my mouth closed and my brain engaged once again, I began to list all of the reasons his idea was ridiculous.

1. I had never done anything like that; I had no experience.
2. I wouldn't even know where to begin.
3. I wouldn't have any idea of where to reach people who would be interested in the same things as I am.
4. I had no background in advertizing or marketing.
5. Even if I had all of the above, I wouldn't know where to go; where would the money come from? Etc., etc.

Howard began his rebuttal to my sound arguments.

1. We had traveled quite a bit by car and already knew where to find some very interesting points of interest. Even though we hadn't planned a trip for a large group before, he reminded me that I certainly had planned many great vacations for smaller groups.
2. Where to begin? There's only one place to begin—at the beginning.
3. He said, "If you, as a Christian, are picky about where you go and what you do, then go talk to other Christians. They probably feel the same way."

4. He reminded me that I could learn how to do it. "I know you can!" he said.

5. Pray about it.

How could I argue with a man like that? So that's what I did; pray about it fervently. I besieged heaven with prayers. "Is this something I really should try to do, Lord?" No answer.

I made inquiries of bus companies on how they based their fees, and they helped me in more ways that words can tell. We took another long weekend to drive to northern Michigan, where we stopped to speak to owners of restaurants and motels, gathering information from them. I kept notes of everything they told me.

After we returned home, I sat down with all my scraps of paper and computed what the cost would probably be, making allowances for mistakes I'd probably make. Once I had an approximate idea of what expenses would be incurred for a busload of possibly forty people, I struggled to arrive at a selling price that would cover the expenditures, break even, and most importantly, please God.

The next step was to come up with a name, register it with the county as a DBA (Doing Business As), have business cards designed, and a variety of necessary papers printed. Ah, there is the rub—money!

Howard, the dear man, told me not to worry; he'd put up the money.

"You can do it; I know you can," he kept telling me.

My prayer life became more intense. *God, why aren't you answering me? I must know that this is something*

You want me to do. Please, God, let a brick building fall on me. I'm scared and I need to know.

I've always believed that God has a sense of humor, and He proved it to me again. Suddenly, the thought came to my mind, *consider the turtle. He never gets anywhere until he sticks his neck out.*

The message was not in King James' words, but I got the point. He *was* behind me, and I must go forth in confidence and faith. All of my other questions were instantly made clear to me.

I must call my business *Jubilee Tours*, for it was to be a holy time, as it says in Leviticus 25:12, "For it is the jubilee; it shall be holy to you." (NKJV)

I also knew I must have a logo of two, crossed silver horns; for it was to be as it was in Numbers 10:1-2. "GOD spoke to Moses: 'Make two bugles of hammered silver. Use them to call the congregation together and give marching orders to the camps.'" (THE MESSAGE)

The horns would be a signal for the crowd to gather and time for the camp to move. I used the same bus company on all my trips. The driver picked up on the symbolism of the horns, and when he was ready to roll, he'd toot his horn twice. It became a standing joke with my regulars. "Toot! Toot! It's time for the camp to move."

I knew I must approach the many churches in my area. With the pastors' permission, I spoke to their retired folks, telling them my dream to have a tour planned to please Christian people. I was to begin and end each day's travel in prayer, and each tour would be a time of fellowship, prayer, and encouragement.

My first trip didn't fill the big bus's capacity of forty-two people. We had thirty-eight in a mixed group of single men and women, couples and widows. One of our scheduled stops was at a Native American church in northern Michigan. I had contacted their pastor, who asked the local elder to meet the bus and speak to our group about the history in the area. While we listened to him, the ladies of the church put out a lovely buffet lunch, and we had a wonderful time of fellowship with them. Despite the protests of the local women, my bus ladies helped clean up after the meal, and a genuine bond was formed in Christian love. We left an appropriate gift for their church as a thank-you for their kindness.

That first trip yielded a small profit for me on which I immediately paid my tithe. That was one thing I knew I had to do.

I continued planning these trips for several years. We visited a Passion Play in Zion, Illinois. We checked into the Hilton Hotel in Chicago overlooking Lake Michigan on Michigan Avenue to spend the night there after the program, on Saturday evening. Sunday morning, our bus took one group to worship services at Moody Memorial Church, and others to Mass at one of the largest Catholic churches in the area. When reunited on the bus again, we headed home, singing hymns and praising God.

Over the years, we made trips to Kentucky, northern Michigan, and many different areas, as well as to the Smokey Mountains for another Passion Play. These experiences were rewarding to me, as they again proved to me the Lord wants to lead us, and He will if we allow Him.

God does have a plan for our lives, and we must learn to trust Him; He will lead us. Consider the turtle.

ALL THINGS RELATIVE

"Relative" means a variety of things to many people. I am thinking in terms of family members—relatives and kinfolks—those to whom we are related by having a common blood tie. The people with whom we are connected by family ties are relatives, but too often that relationship is based on a technicality rather than a sincere, emotional tie.

Theoretically, siblings should have close ties because they share a common blood line. Unfortunately, that's not always true. Blood ties may not be strong enough to overcome differing personality traits.

Then again there are relationships which have fewer genetic reasons which may cause a strong bond between two people, but for some reason, they are tied to each other in a way others may find unusual.

I am thinking of cousins. I have had a total of fifteen cousins. Because of age differences and the distance between our homes, I have been unable to cultivate a warm relationship with all of them. In my growing-up years I was always the youngest, the one whom the more mature ones enjoyed brushing off. I find that I often think of them now and wonder if they ever think of me.

Sadly, I've lost touch with many of my cousins. If we lived nearer to each other I feel confident we would be fast friends and enjoy each other's company. I am thankful for those with whom I have always felt close. It's wonderful to be able to be apart from people for years at a time and suddenly you reconnect. It's as if the years between had never passed. An unexpected phone call or a note is all that is required to renew those deep emotions of love and gratitude for memories from long ago.

I had one boy cousin with whom I always felt close. When he and his wife visited Florida, they would call me, and we'd arrange to meet someplace about halfway between their location and mine. We'd have lunch someplace where we could talk and laugh about the old days and share whatever was predominant in our lives at the time—of recent years it usually was our grandchildren. Those stolen minutes will always be precious to me.

There is still one girl cousin, Gwen, with whom I share that kind of tie. As a little girl I admired her and respected her, and as the years passed those feelings became even stronger. I watched her marry, raise her family, and serve the Lord as they grew.

Recently I was watching the news reports of flooding in her part of the country and decided I needed to call her. We talked for several minutes. She was in North Dakota, and I in Florida, but it felt as if we were sharing the same sofa or having coffee in her kitchen.

We recalled various events in the past. As one memory bounced off another, she reminded me of an event I had completely forgotten. Long after we hung up the phone that night, the memory stuck in my mind.

She had been on one of her visits to Michigan and had made a stop at my mother's apartment. I just lived a couple of blocks away so I rode my recently-purchased bike the short distance to be with them. The three of us had a wonderful visit, laughing and reminiscing about our family members who had gone on.

When it came time for me to head home, I hopped on the bike, confident in my pedaling abilities. However, I had failed to consider the fact that my return trip would be uphill most of the way.

She recalled watching me as I left, pedaling to the corner, making a right turn, and then struggling to make the grade to cross the railroad tracks. She and my mother stood outdoors watching me. I had no idea they'd done that.

Gwen told me my mother kept waving at me and shouting encouragement to me. "You can do it, honey. You can do it. Don't give up!"

Mother turned to Gwen and expressed how very proud she was of me. What a thrill it was for me to hear those words after all these years! I had been so involved in my struggle that I couldn't hear what was said and had no idea of what had happened after I left them. I would never have known if it hadn't been for a chance phone call.

I write all of this because it reminded me of our heavenly Father. When we struggle with our daily life, He is watching us. Can we visualize Him shouting encouragement to us, cheering us on?

"You're doing good. Keep on trying. You're going to make it."

He turns to the angels at His side and tells them how very proud He is as we make efforts to become the strong people He would like us to be.

Just as it is difficult to ride a bike uphill when we first try, each time we do it, it becomes a bit easier. So it is as we struggle to live out our faith. Every hurdle which comes along may be difficult to overcome, but as we succeed with each effort, the next hurdle becomes a bit easier.

There is a saying, "He hasn't brought us this far to let us down now."

We must always remember we are not alone in our struggles in life; we have an Almighty cheering section rooting for us—*onward and upward.*

THE OFFICE ASSISTANT

Have you ever paid close attention to that little creature which appears somewhere on the screen of your PC—the one who looks as if he's made from a paperclip?

As long as I've had this machine, I knew he was there. On occasion, I've called on him to do a spell check or to count words, to print a document, and to save a document.

Today for the first time I looked closely at him. He's got the cutest eyes; they move to watch what I'm doing. I know it sounds silly, but he really does have expressions on his face. His eyebrows move and his eyes change directions. When I stop typing for a while, he even looks as if he's going to sleep, but he will awaken once I begin again.

When I ask him to save a document, he folds himself into a little box, slams the top closed, and then winks at me. If I want to print a document, he coils into a little spring, his eyes rotate, and suddenly my printer comes to life, and the paper with words on it spits out of its opening.

To find out how many words I've typed in a document, he tells me faster than I can think— not only how many words, but also the number of spaces and paragraphs I've completed. When I want to close a document, he asks me if I want to save any changes I've made and if I am really sure this is a task I want him to do. All the time, his eyes become bigger and bigger; his eyebrows go up and down.

Is there something in your life that is so small you really don't notice it? Something which is always ready to do your bidding without complaint, and even ask you if you're really sure that is what you want to do? Have you taken time to say thank you?

God has blessed us in many ways with many things. Even this little critter on the screen of your PC is a blessing. Have you stopped to thank God for him?

No, I'm not being silly. Well, maybe just a little bit. My point is we should take time every day to thank God for the little ways through which He blesses us, whether it is the little office assistant; or the tiny flowers which bloom on the grass in the early hours of the morning; or the sound of a songbird chirping; or the simple fact that we can turn a faucet and water fit for drinking comes gushing forth; or the roof over our heads; or the ample supply of food in our cupboards.

Let us never take for granted the little things which help to make our lives more enjoyable. Never stop thanking God for His bountiful mercies, even the little gizmo which keeps his eyes on our typing. I think he can even blush when I write about him.

REMEMBERING THE WAITING

(A journal entry)

I sit here in my husband's hospital room, waiting. It's two thirty-five in the afternoon on January 24th of 2004. The staff has just taken Howard down to do the C.T. Scan and the Needle Biopsy. They couldn't give me any idea of how long it will take.

This morning, he was in Dialysis. His treatment usually lasts for three hours, but he was gone for almost four and a half hours. I realize the technicians have to do their jobs in a specific manner, and there are only so many machines available. This is a Renal Care Floor, so most of the patients need their turn on the machines. I understand all of that; it's just the waiting.

The Neurosurgeon stopped in and again stressed the urgency of getting the biopsy done A.S.A.P. so they can determine exactly what it is they are up against. Treatment cannot begin until the lab reports are done; they can't even begin the lab work until the biopsy is done; the biopsy cannot be started until he has finished the dialysis. While he sounded urgent about the matter, he also tried to be reassuring.

We didn't understand all the medical terms and the possibilities; perhaps that's just as well. I can get impatient enough with the little I do know. Who knows; if I really understood all of the possibilities the doctors are considering, I might have been in even worse shape than I am right now. It's just the waiting.

This is Saturday afternoon, and the hospital isn't staffed as fully as they are on weekdays.

I'm trying to be patient, Lord. I am trying to be still and know You are here—oh God—I need Your Spirit in a strong and real way right now. I feel very weak and fragile emotionally. I know You are in control of everything; it's just the waiting. . .

The room seems so small and crowded with the two beds. Now with one bed gone, it suddenly feels like a great cavern.

Three thirty p.m. My! Lord, You do act quickly! While I was struggling to feel positive, the nurse came in and said that when Howard comes back to the floor, he'll be put in a private room—number 411.

Lord, You know how much I love the view of the St. Lucie Inlet. Each time we drive over the Roosevelt Bridge and see the beautiful shades of blue in the water and the sky and see the docks with so many boats tied up there, I thank You for making it possible for us to be here. And where is room 411? Overlooking the beauty of the inlet!

I do thank You, Lord. It may seem a small thing to some people, but to me it says that You heard my plea and answered it.

There was really nothing wrong with the other room, but it was a double room, usually full of other people, and with a view of the parking garage. The fountain and little park in front of the hospital is a nice picture, but they don't compare with Your creation of the water, the sky, and the greenery on the opposite shore.

Thank You for hearing me, and thank You for caring. Knowing you are there and that You love me makes the waiting easier.

HEALING OLD WOUNDS

I heard about the man who would be my step-father a long time before I met him. We lived in a very small town where everyone knew everyone else's business, at least in the adult world.

My father had been killed in an auto accident when I was eight, so I grew up in a *single mother* household, long before that term became popular. It was the three of us: my older sister, my mother, and me.

I guess all children feel they are the center of the world, at least I did. I felt when my daddy was killed, I must have done something really bad for God to punish me by taking my daddy away. I became introverted and shy.

There were many aunts and uncles from both sides of the family who tried to be supportive. My dad's family were devout Roman Catholics, and my mother's were sincere Evangelical Christians. Mother fell someplace in between. Looking back over the years, I can see how very innocent a child I was.

Mother met *him* when she bought a new car to replace the one destroyed in Daddy's accident. Even now, after sixty-some years, when I think about those times, the pain is still there. It's sort of like remembering a broken bone; healing has happened, but you just don't forget the pain.

I was used to Mother working; she had for years. I thought that when she started working at *his* office in the evenings, it was for financial reasons; and it probably was in the beginning.

There were times when we would visit either of our extended families, and there would be conversations where voices were lowered for a while, and then Mother's voice would be loud enough for the entire house to hear.

"Mind your own business! It's my life! Girls, get your things; we're leaving! Now!"

When she was in a mood like that, I did what she said with no arguments.

As the years passed, other strange things happened. One day Mother answered a knock on the door. I could see the woman who lived next door to my grandparents, but I couldn't hear what she said.

Suddenly, mother bellowed, "If you're that curious, why don't you just wait nine months to see!" and she slammed the door. I made myself scarce. I didn't understand what it meant, and at the time I didn't want to ask questions.

My sister and I attended grade school at the small, Catholic school. My class was also small—three boys and two girls. My female classmate and I clung to each other. Her mother was a widow too.

When the time came for us to move up to the big high school, we were both nervous about the change. We made a pact that on the first day of school, she would walk to my corner, and then we'd go on to school together. We'd be each other's security blanket.

That September morning, I waited outside for her, when I saw her walking with another girl. As they came to the corner, they didn't cross to my side of the street. They just turned and walked on as if I wasn't there. She didn't speak to me, even though we were in the same classes. I went on, swallowing back the tears that wanted to flow. I learned later that her mother had told her she was to have nothing to do with the daughter of *that woman*.

That afternoon my big sister tried to comfort me. Then she explained to me that mother's extra work and social life was with a married man—a married man whose daughter was also in my sister's class. That's when life taught me that children could be cruel and their parents can be vicious.

My self-esteem dropped to the basement, and the routine of going to school became painful. I never felt the need to work hard to get good grades. I was blessed that I could get A's and B's with little or no effort. When I scored a 155 on an IQ test in ninth grade, mother's reaction was "So?" She didn't expect anything from me so why should I try?

After I met my husband, he too would be happy with whatever I did, so there was little motivation for me to strive to reach higher. Howard had never finished high school. Although mechanically he was a genius, he would modestly brag that anything some fool could put together, he could take apart and fix.

As long as we were married, I never found anything he couldn't fix, redo, or make something that would serve better than the original. However, reading skills were something he just didn't have. I realize now that he was dyslexic. So, when he saw that I could read the entire paper while he struggled with the comic page, he considered me to be much smarter than he was. Of course, he would never encourage me to strive for more.

We married at the end of my junior year, and I expected to be able to graduate with my class. The school board wouldn't let me return to school. They argued I might get pregnant, and then what?

As the years passed, *he* finally was able to get a divorce, and in 1954, he and Mother were married.

Talk about mixed emotions. I felt angry and bitter toward him for the years of gossip and the slights I had to endure. At the same time, I was happy for Mother. It was hard to know how to react, so for a while family relations were strained.

With the babies coming and work being slow for Howard, we were having some difficult financial times early in our marriage. I wanted to get a job to help out, but felt I wasn't trained to do anything, except to cook and clean and care for the babies. Then I began to fret. What would I do if something happened to my husband like it had to my daddy?

I went to the local high school and asked how I could get my GED. I was told they would have to investigate as no one had ever inquired about it before. I finally went to the University of Michigan, and they gave me the General Equivalency Diploma test on which I scored a 99 percentile. The school board came up with a certificate stating I had met all of the requirements of having a high school diploma.

My husband was very supportive, telling me that I was smart enough to do anything I put my hand to. I appreciated that, but it was once again *nobody expects much of me, so why try* syndrome.

I was at my mother's home one day, and I broke into tears, telling her my concerns. He had wakened from his nap, and I didn't know he'd been listening. I heard the footrest of his chair drop, and when I saw him stretch his tall body and walk in my direction, I didn't know how to react.

He put his huge arms around me so that my cheek was pressed tightly against his shirt buttons, and he told me, "Honey, you can do anything you can think you can do. You've got a fine mind, and if you study, you can learn anything you want to learn. All you have to do is *want to* badly enough."

He then asked me what I'd like to do, and I wasn't sure what to say, so I blurted out, "I like to work with numbers." In school, when I'd expressed my desire to write, I was mocked and sneered at. So we began a course of learning bookkeeping at the kitchen table. He crammed my head full of more information than I ever dreamed I could learn.

He had been a schoolteacher in his youth, and then became a Chrysler dealer. He taught me the corporation's system and told me with that knowledge I could get any job I ever wanted. He told me that I have been made "special" and that I had been given gifts and abilities other people weren't given, and they may have talents and abilities that I wasn't given.

He gave me the self-confidence and the motivation to go out and try to do the things I thought I couldn't do. His support and encouragement changed my life from being a timid house mouse to someone who is not afraid to speak in front of a group of people or to take a chance on something in which I believe.

As I look back, I can see where in the years between then and now those gifts have been used to serve and honor God by leading in Bible studies, helping in the administrative duties of my church's office, and even in the writing I do to entertain myself.

He encouraged me as I started a small travel business of my own, which I ran for over five years with the self-confidence he'd given me. I took an active part in my community, helping to start our local food bank, and serving as Secretary on the Board of Directors for five years. I went from that to helping with setting up a hospice program for our community.

Imagine that! Me—working with degreed professional people, and I held up my end by typing all of the Policies and Procedures, and then doing all of the Medicare Billing. As our program merged with our local hospital, I continued doing the hospice billing until I was able to retire, grandfathered into the hospital's retiree insurance program.

He stopped being *him* and became the stepfather I loved like my own father. When he died suddenly in that same recliner chair in 1971, I felt I had lost a father, a mentor, a teacher, and a friend because he had made a big difference in my life.

He was an admirable man, but compared to Jesus, he was nothing. In the early stage of my Christian growth, God used many people like him to show me that God had given me special gifts or talents which others may or may not have, and He expects me to use those gifts in His service.

I have to thank the man who made a difference in my life. More importantly, I must remember to thank the Man who by showing me His love, made my life here bearable and the future life even more wonderful than I could imagine.

Thank you to my stepfather; but primarily, thank you, Jesus.

ANCHORS AND RUDDERS

Over the years, my husband had many boats of varying sizes. I learned a lot of things from them—things which have also helped me in my day-to-day life.

I learned the importance of having a good anchor. For example, did you know that there are many different types and sizes of anchors? There are anchors which look much like a button mushroom. They are made of heavy material and vary in size. They are best used when the bottom of the water is mucky or muddy. They settle into the bottom and stay put.

Some anchors are a long bar, hinged at the bottom with two finger-like sections which move. This type of anchor is best used where the bottom of the water is covered with rocks. When this anchor is dropped, it may drag a bit, but suddenly, the fingers will grab hold of the rocks and will keep the boat from moving any further. The larger the rocks, the larger the anchor should be.

Other anchors are like the ones we often see on yacht-owners caps. They have a long bar, with a cross bar near the top. On the bottom there is a crescent shaped bar with barbs on each end. This type is pretty much a multi-use anchor so the boater doesn't need to carry along several different ones.

There is another anchor, which you may have never seen. It's called a sea anchor. It looks a little like a large fabric bag or the drogue chute on a racecar. It's generally used to slow the forward speed of the boat or to help it maintain a straight-line course. Under certain conditions a boat may "yaw" or swerve back and forth. This makes maintaining a course next to impossible.

Dragging a sea anchor helps the pilot to hold his course.

Whatever the size or shape of the anchor, they all have an important job to do. They must hold the boat in a certain location.

The rudder of the boat is another vital tool. Whether it is a small sailing vessel or a large ocean-going vessel, the rudder is the only thing which keeps the ship maneuverable and steerable.

In order for the rudder to work, water must move across its surface. Whether it moves by the forward motion of the boat or as the water itself moves, there must be movement for it to do its job.

The vessel's navigator, or pilot, can by the movement of one finger order it to be moved in one direction or another, or to be held steady, which determines the direction in which the vessel will move. The pilot in control of the rudder is the most vital part of the vessels. Without the two of them working in harmony, the ship can be driven to the rocks and destroyed.

My husband always wore one piece of jewelry, a Mariner's Cross, on a chain around his neck. When anyone would ask him about it, he would give his reply. "I wear this cross as a reminder that Jesus is the pilot of my ship of life; He is the One who guides and steers me. My faith in Jesus is 'the anchor of my soul; both sure and steadfast.'" (Hebrews 6:19 NKJV). He would continue to say that his anchor goes through the veil directly to the throne of God, which is a loose paraphrase of the rest of that verse.

Do you have a good anchor? Who is piloting your ship? Jesus is ready and willing to handle the task for you.

ARCHIE AND LIZZIE CHAMBERLAIN

When I was about ten or twelve during World War II, I was able to spend several months on a farm owned by friends of my mother's, Archie and Lizzie Chamberlain. I never did know why I was taken there during the school year. My sister went to visit an aunt and uncle at the same time. Mother worked and stayed home. I guess *why* will always be a bit of a mystery.

Farm life was totally different from any way I had ever lived. Having grown up in a small town, I was able to walk to school, stores, church or the movies. This farm was remote, and trips to town were carefully planned—not only due to distance or the time it would take, but also because gasoline was being rationed.

While there I was introduced to many aspects of farming. I learned about plowing and tilling fields from atop a big, old horse; my legs ached for several days after straddling her.

Another thing I learned was hog butchering. I helped to prepare the meat for preserving. As I watched how *head cheese* was made, I determined that was one thing I would never sample.

I had the opportunity to learn many things in Lizzie's kitchen too. We made pickles, and canned fruits and vegetables for use the next winter. I think the big iron stove on which she made marvelous meals fascinated me the most. The stove used wood for fuel. I had never seen such a thing before. At home we had an apartment sized gas stove with three burners.

I'd watch her bake pies and cakes, bread and biscuits, and prepare meals. Looking back, I'm amazed she was able to maintain a steady temperature, never burned anything, nor did she present anything not thoroughly cooked.

On the back of the cook top was a small, closed area she called "warming ovens." On the extreme right side of the oven was a large tank she kept full of water. Thanks to that, she always had about five gallons of hot water available, not on tap, but on hand.

When the cook top cooled down, she would take the wrapper from store-bought bread and use it as a polishing cloth. The wax in it made the surface shine.

Sunday was, of course, church day. I had no problem dressing appropriately, but was shocked to see what Archie called church attire. He wore sparkling clean, bib-top overalls with a neatly starched and ironed white shirt, complete with necktie. He wore his working boots made of heavy rubber, which came just below his knees. He would wash and polish them, but even so, I sort of stared at him, as he wore his pants tucked inside the boots. His coat (today they'd call it a "barn coat") was of heavy denim, lined with some sort of heavy material that resembled a blanket. I can't forget the tattered, old hat. I'm sure it was a handsome fedora when it was new, but it had seen many years of hard use.

I recall one particular Sunday when Archie and a visiting evangelist stood on the porch, after the service, arms locked and singing, *Give Me That Old Time Religion*. They kept time by stomping their feet in unison. I thought they were a bit strange. I soon discovered it was my first exposure to the Holy Spirit in action.

Looking back now, I realize they were actually living Psalm 32:11. "Be glad in the Lord, and rejoice, ye righteous; and shout for joy, all ye that are upright in heart." (KJV). They were so transported with holy joy they weren't able to contain themselves. They affected others with their joy, for they could see that a life of communion with the Lord could be the most pleasant and comfortable life we could live in this world. These men were proud to show their love for the Lord publicly.

I was there in the late summer when the wheat and oats were ready to harvest, so I learned what it means to be "hungry as threshers." This team of neighbors and the man who owned the big threshing machine arrived before eight a.m. and quickly went to work in the big fields.

Even before they arrived, Lizzie kept me busy helping her to prepare the noon meal. Such a meal! When the crew came to the house for the noonday meal, Lizzie had made a place by the back door with a bench, a pair of basins and several towels where they could wash up. She also had pitchers of lemonade and ice water set out so they could wash down the dust from their work. While they did that, she and I put the food on a huge table set for ten or more men.

Archie asked a blessing on the food before they all sat down.

They feasted on fried chicken, mashed potatoes, gravy, fresh sweet corn, fresh tomatoes and green peppers, pickled cucumbers and onions. All of these were products from their farm, not store bought.

Biscuits, still warm from the oven, hand-churned butter, and gallons of coffee (at least it seemed to me like gallons), as well as the water and lemonade completed the feast.

As one bowl was emptied, it was my job to take it to the kitchen to be refilled. When I'd get back to the table, another bowl would be emptied. Once they slowed down and were talking and laughing, the deserts came out—warm apple and cherry pies with fresh, heavy cream poured all over them.

Soon I'd hear the noise of chairs being pushed back across the wooden floor as they returned to the fields to finish their job. After they left, Lizzie would tell me to fix myself something to eat. Even if there had been leftovers, I was too tired to eat. I helped her clean up, do the dishes, and when she told me to go take a nap, I didn't argue with her about it.

Of all those memories, I think the most precious one is helping Archie at *sugar time*. It was spring; the thaw began; new life returned; buds began to pop; and the sap rose in the maple trees.

Archie hooked the team to a thing he called a *mud boat*. It looked like a big raft on two long skids, which curved up in front. Every day we would ride into the woods on that thing over mud and snow and followed the trail of trees he had tapped earlier. Tapping consisted of a special little instrument that he hammered into the trees from which he could hang a bucket into which the sap would run.

When we had completed the loop, we'd have several buckets filled with a clear liquid a bit thicker than water. Then it was time to go to the *sugar shack*. In there were several huge tubs over a fire which he would keep burning for several days at a time. Each bucket was emptied into one of the tubs. The tubs were filled at different times so that each was in process of cooking down at a different rate. As the liquid simmered slowly, he skimmed off the foam which rose to the top, and then he discarded it.

One day, he poured about a one-cup ladle full of that stuff over the freshly fallen snow. "Try that," he told me.

I gingerly scooped it up and tested it; it was delicious—better than any ice cream I'd ever had before or since.

When it had reached a certain point— he was the only one who knew what that point was—he filled a huge, clean jug using the ladle and a metal funnel, and brought it into the house. I don't know how big that jug was, but at the time it looked like more than a gallon to me. A lot of work had gone into making that one jug of syrup.

Lizzie would heat it to the right temperature on that old stove, and then pour it into various sizes of glass jars and bottles, and sealed them with wax. Homemade maple syrup! Such a luxury. She told me friends and neighbors would bring empty glass containers to her, knowing they would get at least one bottle back filled with fresh maple syrup with no additives.

One night when it began to storm violently, I came to understand just how much their lives were totally different than I could ever have imagined. About midnight, Lizzie came to my room and told me to get up and get dressed. I had been sleeping soundly and wasn't even aware of the storm. When I entered the dining room, they were sitting at the table. I could see her purse beside her, and she pointed for me to sit down.

I asked why we were up, and she said it was so we could watch the storm. I thought that was a bit strange, but I didn't argue. Archie read from the Bible until the lights went out. Suddenly a ball of fire flew out of their wooden, wall-hung, hand-crank telephone. It went past me, and then vanished.

When daylight broke, we all went outside to see what had happened. We learned that a tornado had gone through the area, and several nearby homes had been destroyed.

Archie and Lizzie were a dear couple, and I will never forget them or the times I spent with them. When I was married, it surprised me to discover that so many of the lessons she had taught me in her kitchen would become a vital part of my life.

Decades later, as we watched the TV program, *Little House on the Prairie*, I couldn't help but remember those two, gentle folks. Their home was a few years removed from the story, but not by much, and I'm grateful that I had the chance to know and learn from them.

I also learned to appreciate their simple lifestyle and to treasure the memories, especially the experience of watching them live their faith in God on a daily basis.

ARE YOU LISTENING?

In the winter of 1976 our oldest daughter, who at that time lived near Lexington, Kentucky, was rushed to the hospital. The doctor said her appendix was severely infected and was on the verge of rupturing.

It didn't take us long to pack and prepare to make the trip from our home in Michigan. We arrived at the hospital about six or seven hours after we had received the call.

As fortune would have it, her mother-in-law had been visiting at the time, so she was able to stay at home with our three grandchildren. Grateful for that blessing, we were able to spend our time at the hospital to await the surgeon's report.

He looked grim as he spoke with her husband and us. "She's a very sick girl, but she'll be fine in time."

He marveled that her appendix was enlarged. With his fingers, he showed us that it was about six inches long and one and a half inches across. "That's not all," he added. "There were thirty-some tumors in it. All except three were malignant. We got them all and she will be fine. Oh, by the way, her appendix was on the wrong side of her abdomen."

You can imagine the relief and the joy we felt. At the same time a parent's guilt set in. When she was much younger, she often complained of pain in her abdomen. The doctors made little of it, and we told her that it couldn't be her appendix because it was on the other side. What kind of a parent would not pick up on that? I remember walking the halls of the hospital,

233

trying to convince myself that I really hadn't been a neglectful mother. I could only make decisions on her condition based on the information I had at the time. It wasn't working, though. The guilt stayed with me.

We expressed our appreciation to the doctor.

"Don't thank me. Thank God that she lived this long!"

We did just that. The next few days were full. We spent most of the daytime at the hospital with her while the other grandmother stayed with the children.

One morning as I stood outside of the door to her room, one of the housekeeping ladies was busy cleaning the floor of the hall. As she moved her large dust mop back and forth, she hummed a gospel song. Then she began to sing the words.

HOW LONG HAS IT BEEN?

How long has it been, since you talked to the Lord,
And told Him your heart's hidden secrets?
How long since you prayed,
How long since you stayed,
On your knees 'til the light shone through?
How long has it been since your mind felt at ease,
How long since your heart knew no burden?
Can you call Him your friend,
How long has it been,
Since you knew that He cared for you?
How long has it been since you knelt by your bed,
And prayed to the lord up in heaven?
How long since you knew,
That he'd answer you,
And would keep you the long night through?

How long has it been since you woke with the dawn,
And felt that the day's worth the living?
Can you call Him your friend,
How long has it been,
Since you knew that He cared for you?[3]

Long after she was discharged from the hospital and we all had returned to our homes, that song stuck in my mind. It had been quite some time since I had really talked to God, and even longer since I had listened for His reply.

I had been watching the P.T.L. Club on TV when one morning in April of that year, someone on the program sang that song. Then the Lord touched my heart through the speaker.

I had always been the kind of person who was very religious. I had known all about God and had read the Bible and knew many of His stories. But I had never met Him as I did that morning! I remember falling to my knees and crying out to God, asking His forgiveness for my sin of neglecting Him for religion, and for all of the sins that followed after that. That morning I claimed all of His promises made through the sacrifice of His Son, Jesus.

That was the beginning of a new life for me—a total commitment of my life to honor and serve Him. That doesn't mean I immediately became perfect. No, I

---

[3]*How Long Has It Been,*1956© Southern Faith Songs Administered by THE COPYRIGHT COMPANY. NASHVILLE, TN, Mosie Lister Songs All Rights Reserved. International Copyright Secured. Used by Permission

was still the same woman with the same human nature, but I had surrendered to God the possession of my life, my will, and my soul.

That was over thirty years ago, and since then I have grown and matured in His love. I prayed that people around me can see the difference between me today and the "B.C. me" (Before Christ).

As the old saying goes, "I'm not perfect; I'm forgiven," and I am listening to His voice more.

SOMETHING'S OUT THERE!

In the early days of our marriage, we would often go for a drive with friends. Sometimes we would start directly after the men left work, but usually it would be after supper. One couple would pick up the other, and then we would just drive around the countryside.

We were usually ready to call it a day not long after dark. The men always had to make a "pit stop" somewhere along the trip. The area around us was still very rural, wooded and relatively wild, so they thought nothing of stopping on a back road and going behind a bush or a tree.

My husband was usually the last to finish. On one occasion, we wondered what was keeping him, when suddenly my husband came rushing to the car. Breathless, he jumped in and slammed the door.

"There's something out there!" he gasped.

Curious, we rolled the windows down a bit to be able to hear anything in the night. After a few minutes, we heard it too. Something was crashing around in the brush.

The road being too narrow to make a turn, the driver had to drive a bit until he came to an entrance used by a farmer to go into his fields. He turned the car around, and using his big spotlight, he carefully inspected the bushes and brush on the side of the road.

He suddenly stopped and laughed. There in the glare of his big light, stood and old bull. He wasn't something one would care to meet in the daylight, much less after dark.

We all joined in the laughter, especially my husband. He was too aware of what an unhappy bull could do if he were so inclined to do something.

It was a fun experience, but it was a life lesson too. Things may be going smoothly with no problems, but beware. Trouble may just be over the fence.

1Peter 5:8 tells us to "Be sober, be vigilant, because your adversary the devil walks about like a roaring lion, seeking who he may devour." (NKJV)

SILLY BIRDS! WHY ARE YOU WALKING?

Living in Florida, we see wild birds which have made themselves very much at home wherever they are. Sandhill Cranes, Snowy Egrets, and many other varieties like to wander through our subdivision, picking in the grass for worms and other tasty items to eat.

It is understood that when the birds are in the street, they have the right of way. It isn't unusual to see a family of cranes holding up traffic for several minutes at a time while they amble around undecided on which direction to chose.

One Sunday as I was on my way home from church, I turned off the busy highway to the corner of my street, and there were several Egrets, casually strolling across the road. I stopped and the car behind me stopped just in the nick of time. As I watched impatiently, I muttered to the birds.

"You silly birds! Why are you walking when God gave you wings so you can fly?"

My impatience didn't hustle them along one little bit. As I watched them boldly meander along, the thought came to mind, *how many times in my life have I walked when I could have been flying? When I could have been rejoicing and praising God, why did I mope and complain about my lot?*

I decided then to follow the advice given us in Psalm 118:24. "This is the day the Lord has made; **let us rejoice and be glad in it**." (NIV; bold is by author for emphasis.)

TRUSTING GOD, IN SPITE OF IT ALL

My devotional thought for the day had been *Praying in God's will*. The theme of the lesson was how sometimes it is easy to trust God for the big things, but the little things can trip us up. Trusting is something we develop as we grow in our walk with Him.

The day before had been a busy one with several errands to be run, and it was exceptionally hot, even for Florida. I had just finished the last task and was putting the milk and ice cream in the car. I was so grateful that in a few minutes I would go from my air-conditioned car to my air-conditioned home.

As I turned the key, I heart that click-click sound—the sound of a dead battery! My mind raced. *I don't have any idea of who to call for help! What will I do?*

I was seconds away from panic, but instead, I prayed. "Lord, help me."

Then His peace settled over me. I called the dealer where I had bought the car. They didn't have road service, but she gave me the number for the company they used. I called that number and was told the truck was in my area and would be there in a few minutes.

The store manager had noticed my situation and took the perishables I'd purchased back into the store to keep them in the cooler until I was ready for them.

In less than fifteen minutes, my car was running again, the perishables were in my back seat, and I was on my way home to put them away. From there, I went directly to the dealership to have them check out the engine.

The problem was a bad voltage regulator, which had shorted out the battery. They had to have parts delivered, and they told me the car would be ready in the morning, so they gave me a loaner car. I got home less than an hour later.

The next morning, they called to tell me the car was ready. The total was $383.00. The good news was that the extended warranty I had purchased when I bought the car covered the cost. Thank You, Lord!

"Now this is the confidence that we have in Him, that if we ask anything according to His will, He hears us. And if we know that He hears us, whatever we ask, we know that we have the petitions that we have asked of Him." (NKJV)

WEARING MASKS

An article I read in my devotional book brought back many memories of the times when our children were small. The writer encouraged people to allow their families and friends to be honest with them—to be able to express their opinions to them freely.

I couldn't help but recall the terrible times when we tried to get five children ready to go someplace. I usually ended up getting a terrible headache, being nauseous, and quite often, just staying home.

One time my husband took me to a doctor to learn why I had these headaches. The doctor asked when they usually came on, and the answer was whenever we were getting ready to go somewhere. His profound opinion was that perhaps I really didn't want to go.

I stormed out of his office, muttering to myself that if he had ever tried to get five children and a husband all ready to go at the same time he'd get a headache too.

But he did make me stop to think about it. The very worst times were on Sunday morning as we prepared to leave for church. There would be a chorus of, "My hair looks terrible. I just can't go!"

"I can't find my shoes."

"Can't you all stop yelling?"

When we did get to church, as we'd leave the car someone would call out to us, "Isn't this a lovely day?"

"How are you all today?"

243

"We're all just fine, thanks." We had put up our masks, and on the surface everything looked nice and pleasant.

Sometimes we go farther than just wearing a mask. We build walls to keep others out. We fear that if others really knew us as we really are, they wouldn't accept us.

I remember an old preacher once saying to his congregation, "If you all really knew me as I am, you wouldn't be sitting there listening to me. If I really knew you all as you really are, I probably wouldn't speak to you. But God knows us as just exactly as we are, and He loves us anyway. Can we do less?"

Isn't it wonderful when you can have a relationship with someone and feel so secure that you can tell them anything about yourself and not worry about shocking them or that they will repeat every word you said to someone they know?

Wearing masks might be compared to wearing a veil. Masks hide one's identity, but they often make it difficult to see what is going on around us.

In Genesis, it tells of Moses wearing a veil. He did so to keep the people from seeing his face. He had seen God and His glory was shown on Moses' face. The people were unable to see that glory. The story later speaks of them having veils on their hearts.

Today, the Jews are not only the ones who have veils on their hearts, which keep them from seeing the glory of Jesus and the work He did for us, because he loves us.

In 2 Corinthians 3:18, we can read where it says that "We all", with unveiled faces can see our faces shining with the brightness of His face. It also tells us that we will gradually become more and more like Him. (Author's paraphrase)

If we ask, Jesus is more than able to take those veils away. If we will turn to the Lord, He will take away the veil, and we can be one of the "we all." God will change our lives, and change us from the inside-out.

The best and most enduring change comes into our lives when we are transformed by time spent with the Lord. There are many other ways to change, but none of them are as deep and long-lasting as the transformation that comes by the Spirit of God as we spend time in the presence of the Lord.

YOU CAN FOOL SOME OF THE PEOPLE

Several years ago we had a cat. This feline had a unique personality and made a definite spot for himself in my husband's heart. We all liked him, but as far as my husband was concerned, Henry was the world's best cat.

Henry loved to run free in the country, chasing squirrels, rabbits and little girl cats. He would run at night, but by five thirty in the morning, he was always at the front door waiting for my husband to let him in.

After one of his little excursions, Henry came to the door, but he just lay there, unmoving even after we opened the door. After examining him, we discovered that his left rear leg had been broken. There was no way to tell what had caused his injury.

Of course, we had to bundle him up and take him to the vet. Henry was unique and deserved to be properly cared for, even at the expense of a veterinary bill. The vet kept him overnight, set his leg, put it in a cast, and made a crutch for him out of aluminum tubing.

He presented quite a picture when we brought him home. My husband made a little nest beside his chair, and that's where he recuperated. After several days of TLC, my husband decided it was time for Henry to attempt to walk on his crutch.

Although the cat managed to look pitiful, the master knew that he must walk again on his own, or he would never heal properly. After a few days of struggling, Henry managed to learn his own unique style of walking on his crutch. After a few weeks he was almost able to run on it.

The time came when the bone was healed, the crutch was taken off, and the cast removed. That presented a genuinely pitiful sight. A cat's leg is not muscular, and to see it shaved bald and skinny—well, it was unique.

The cat was able to fool Howard for nearly a month after his leg healed. We told him Henry could walk normally when Howard wasn't around, but it was just too much for the man to believe. As much as he cared for Henry, he vowed no cat could ever pull the wool over his eyes.

Henry had his master's work schedule figured out. He knew when it was time for him to go to work, and when it was time for him to come home for supper. When Henry hadn't planned on was the one time Howard decided to come home a few hours early.

My husband hadn't been feeling well, so he went straight to his Lazy-Boy chair, put up his feet, and was resting with his eyes open. Henry strolled through the living room at his usual brisk pace, and as he passed the big chair, my husband looked down to see him walking without a limp.

"You faker!" he cried, and the footrest came down suddenly. Henry took one look at him, began to limp away, and then stopped. He knew the jig was up. The family gathered around them, laughing hysterically, but man and cat just stared at each other.

There is a place in the book of Job that teaches this subject in chapter 12:16-17. "Strength and success belongs only to God; both the deceived and the deceiver must answer to Him." (THE MESSAGE)

Man decided to go back to his comfortable chair, the cat decided to settle down on his lap, and the standoff was ended.

A LITTLE CHILD SHALL
LEAD THEM

In the early days of my walk with the Lord, I began to realize how much I had to learn and how much I had to unlearn. As part of my religious life, I felt that anything connected to God must be solemn, straitlaced, and dignified, as well as quiet.

As I became familiar with the idea that God really loved me, and that He was truly my heavenly Father, I grew fascinated as I watched some Christian TV programs. These people who truly loved the Lord behaved in a manner in which I thought was unseemly, even though I enjoyed watching them.

They would stand with their eyes closed and raise their outstretched hands. This type of worship, I learned later, was considered *Pentecostal.* I had been attending church at a local Baptist congregation, and when I mentioned watching this on TV, one of the pastors asked me if I was "one of those charismatics." I couldn't answer him because I wasn't certain just what a charismatic was, so I just said, "No, I'm not."

I decided this was one subject I would have to study and learn for myself. That began my Bible study of the words *prayer* and *hands.* I was truly shocked to see that the Old Testament was full of references to people raising their hands in prayer.

The more I studied, the more I watched those TV programs and I began to realize this behavior did honor the Lord.

I prayed in earnest, asking Him to show me exactly what He would prefer—what would truly honor

Him. I went from church to church, seeking His leading.

One day our oldest son and his little girls stopped by for a quick visit. As usual, he checked my cupboards. He stood munching on potato chips, when the littlest girl came up to him and reached out her arms to him.

Well, I didn't need a brick building to fall on me after that. She didn't need to use words; she wasn't even talking yet. But she was able to communicate to her daddy that she wanted some of his chips.

If raising her hands to her daddy worked so well for her, why should I hesitate to use the same method? Jesus said something to the effect that a little child shall lead them. Well, what He said was, "Unless you return to square one and start over like children, you're not even going to get a look at the kingdom, let alone get in." (Mathew 18:3, THE MESSAGE)

UNCLE BILL'S WEDDING

I was a little over four years old when my mother's youngest brother got married. It was a beautiful ceremony, and rather fancy for the days of the mid-1930's. As I recall the whole thing took place at the home of his new in-laws, a large farm northeast of Fowlerville, Michigan. The big lawn, the flowers, and blooming shrubs created a beautiful setting. What I remember most is the reception after the ceremony.

As a child, I couldn't understand why everybody stood around, talking and taking pictures. The bride was so beautiful in her gown and veil; the three young women who were her attendants looked lovely too. I kept running into the house, where I knew there was cake and ice cream just waiting to be eaten.

Finally, my mother stopped me, gave me her favorite discipline by pinching my earlobe, and told me to calm down, or else! I went into the big room where most of the adults were sitting and took a seat, at least for a while.

They began to serve the cake and ice cream. I don't remember who was doing the serving. I remember several ladies brought plates of cake and ice cream and handed them to the adults, one at a time. They passed me by, and I figured that maybe they didn't see me, so I went into the next room.

The same pattern was repeated there; again I was passed by. I went into the next room, which was beside the kitchen where the food was being put onto the plates. Once again, they forgot me. I broke into tears and ran out the door to hide underneath a big shade tree.

In time, my mother came looking for me. She was upset with me, as usual because by this time my face was tear streaked, my nose was running, and my dress was terribly wrinkled. She calmed me down and asked me what on earth was wrong.

As I sniffled and sobbed I explained to her that I didn't get any cake or ice cream—that I had been completely overlooked.

I thought surely she would understand and sympathize with me. I was wrong.

Instead of pity, I was given a lecture about how it might not have happened that way if I had done as I was told to do, which was go sit down and stay there.

As it turned out, my uncle had become aware of the situation, and as soon as he could get away from the adults, he came out to me, carrying a plate of cake and ice cream, which he handed to me.

He said that he remembered what it was like to be the littlest kid in a crowd of adults. He shooed Mother back inside, telling her to not say another word, and he sat beside me under the big tree, and talked to me as if I were a grownup. I don't remember how long we were out there before his new bride came looking for him, but I do remember that for the first time in my life, someone other than my daddy made me feel special.

Many years later, I was to learn that my heavenly Father, my Abba Father, my Daddy God, made me to be special. In Jeremiah 1:5, he said that before we are formed in our mother's womb, God knew us. In Exodus 33:12 & 17, He said that He knows us by name.

I learned also that there are times when I must just be still and wait for Him to move in my life; there will be times when I must abide in Him. If I do that, "He will abide in me". (John 15:7)

BAD HABITS AND BREAKING TIMES

In 1963 I kept busy caring for five children, one husband and one grandfather in his late eighties. In addition to them, I tried to be a peacemaker between the grandfather and his daughter, who happened to also be my mother-in-law. This lady did not make the job easy. I wondered if the two of them could ever have a good relationship.

It seemed as if the world were crashing in on me. The doctor told my husband that he should get me away from the stress, or I'd end up in a hospital. Even the thought of trying to get ready to go away put a whole new series of stresses on me.

The old gentleman decided it would be better for all concerned if he were to find another place to stay, and the mother-in-law thought this idea was an outrage. They argued about that, and she determined that if he were to leave, it would be her duty to move in with us to help care for the children. Now that was a scary thought!

To make a long story short, we did get away from home for a few days. When we returned, she was ready to get back to her own home.

While we were gone, my husband suggested if I were to smoke a few cigarettes a day, it might help with my nerves. So I tried that. I nearly choked to death on the first few, but after I graduated to the menthol flavored cigarettes, it became easier. By the time 1976 rolled around, the few a day had turned into two packs a day.

In April of that year I committed my life to the Lord, but continued the nasty habit. Midsummer that year, I decided the living room needed to be painted—no small project.

On the second day of that undertaking, after everyone had gone and I was ready to get back to the job, I discovered I didn't have enough cigarettes to last for the day. A big decision needed to be made; should I go to the store before I started painting, or paint awhile and then go?

I stood in the middle of the room in my jeans and one of my husband's old work shirts, trying to make the choice. I muttered to myself, "Why did I ever start this habit? Oh, that's right. It was to help my nerves."

Suddenly, behind me I heard a powerful, resonant voice speak these words, "My grace is sufficient for thee."

I turned around to see who had spoken, and found myself still alone in the house. I must admit, there are times when I am slow to understand things, but that morning I got the message loud and clear.

Immediately, I emptied all the ashtrays, washed them, and put them in a cupboard. I went to work and was able to finish the job that day without the need or craving for nicotine.

My family had been on me to quit for several months, but I determined not to say anything to them about quitting. I didn't want to give them the satisfaction of thinking they had talked me into it.

The next few days, the toxins which had built up in my body came out of every pore and opening. I coughed up and sneezed out nasty goo, perspired more than ever before in my life, my ears drained something, and I suffered from severe diarrhea and other heavy body discharges. But there were no symptoms of withdrawal pains and no craving for the nicotine.

A few days later, I happened onto an open pack left in a purse, and my stingy nature (we know who it was) told me to just smoke them and not to waste them. I lit one, and it tasted worse than the first one I'd had over thirteen years before. All I could think was, "My grace is sufficient for thee." The pack and its contents went into the fireplace, fast.

After two weeks, I finally had a withdrawal symptom. I threw a hissy fit at my husband and kids.

"All of you have been on me to stop smoking, and for two weeks I haven't had one cigarette, and you haven't even noticed!" Well, I didn't just stop there, but I managed to make them all feel shame that they hadn't noticed or said anything to me.

That was the only time I ever physically heard the voice of my God. He had a very real, powerful voice. I knew when I heard it exactly who was speaking to me. Since then, there have been times when He whispers in my ear or puts thoughts into my mind, but never again have I heard that voice.

I know that one day I will hear it again—when He meets me and says, "Well done, good and faithful servant. Welcome home!"

I LOVE YOU BECAUSE

When we managed a getaway in 1963, my husband took me to the shores of Lake Michigan to a town named Ludington. One of our favorite places to eat was an old-fashioned diner east of town on Highway 10. Every picture which comes to mind when you think of an old-fashioned diner would apply to that place in those days—black and white tile on the floor, a big jukebox, and individual selectors at each table and booth. I don't remember if it took nickels or quarters to operate.

My husband was never one to play jukeboxes; he wasn't really a music fan at all. But there was one song he liked so well, he kept feeding coins into the machine—so many coins that it played the whole time we were there, and probably for a while after we left.

My husband was not an overtly emotional person, nor one to express his affections. Once early in our marriage in 1948, I asked him if he loved me.

"I married you, didn't I?" he replied. "If anything changes, I'll tell you."

However, that day he did tell me it was the only song he ever heard which expressed how he felt about me. He said all of this as he held my hand across the table. Puddle up time!

For the rest of our years together, every time we heard that song, we went back in time to that little diner in 1963 and the emotions would be renewed. That song became special to us, and I had it played during Howard's "going home celebration."

Leon R. Payne wrote the words and music in 1958. Unfortunately, he died in 1969, but I really want to give credit to him because he certainly deserves it.

Many years have passed since that day. I still love to listen to that song, no matter who is singing it. I realized recently that it also expressed for me the feeling I have toward the Lord.

If you stretch your imagination, you can also sing it as a love song to the Lord. Mr. Payne, bless you for the joy and peace your words bring to my mind.

"I love you because you understand, dear
Every single thing I try to do.
You're always there to lend a helping hand, dear.
I love you most of all because you're you.
No matter what the world may say about me,
I know your love will always see me through.
I love you for the way you never doubt me.
But most of all, I love you 'cause you're you.
I love you because my heart is lighter
Since I've been walking by your side.
I love you because my future's brighter
The door to happiness you open wide.
No matter what the world may say about me
I know your love will always see me through.
I love you for a hundred thousand reasons.
But most of all, I love you 'cause you're you.[4]
To this, I say a hearty Amen!

HOW MANY FOR LUNCH?

Living in Michigan in the winter presents many varying forms of entertainment: skating, skiing, sledding, and one of our favorites, snowmobiling. Whichever sport one chooses, the first prerequisite is a good, warm wardrobe; warm boots, layers of clothing, gloves, facemasks, and if snowmobiles are your choice, a helmet is a good safety factor.

We lived in the country where it was possible to take our machines out of a warm garage, cross the road, and go many miles and never run on a roadway. There were uncounted acres of land which the state had purchased, and many more were just sitting there, waiting for a land developer to come along to fill them with houses.

Our friends who lived in town brought their machines to our house and left them there, just waiting for a chance for a ride. On weekends, it wasn't unusual for there to be fifteen or twenty machines sitting in our front yard. We weren't always sure who owned them at first, but as time passed, we found we had new friends.

Weekends, it became standard procedure for me to make a huge kettle of chili and another of soup. The big coffee maker was always ready to go too. We got the reputation of holding "open house," and no one ever took advantage of our hospitality.

The soup, chili, and coffee were always set up in the dining room, along with the appropriate dishes, mugs, spoons, and "go-withs." Next to them, we put a little bowl, and as people would help themselves to lunch, they would drop money in the bowl to help cover the expenses. We never asked anyone to pay for the food, but somehow, the money in the bowl usually covered the costs.

It seemed everyone knew my husband had everything to work with in his garage, and again, it was not unusual to have a total stranger in there with him, trying to solve a problem with his machine.

All of this happened during the period of time when I was first growing in the Lord. These people never showed up on a Sunday morning because they knew I would be in church, and they respected that. Occasionally one of the ladies would join me at church on a Sunday evening.

For the times when it was just too cold to be outdoors, the men gathered in our basement around the pool table. Later I learned my husband told them about the Lord while they played. Those who were uncomfortable with it left, but some stayed and listened.

Now that I live in Florida, I think back to those days and I can't help but wonder, "Were we out of our minds? Riding a snowmobile in temperatures in the teens or twenties, if not colder, at night as well as during the day?" I guess it's a good thing we were much younger then.

I'm grateful for the memories of those days, and even more thankful I may never have to be cold again!

Recalling those days, I think of 1Peter 4:8-10. "Love each other as if your life depended on it. Love makes up for practically anything. Be quick to give a meal to the hungry; a bed to the homeless—cheerfully. Be generous with the difficult things God gave you, let it be God's words; if help, let it be God's hearty help.

That way, God's bright presence will be evident in everything through Jesus." (THE MESSAGE)

It was after Howard's death that I began to learn the many ways my husband had ministered to different men, encouraging them to save their marriages or helping them in other ways to grow and become strong, respectable men.

If seeds were sown via kettles of soup or cups of coffee, I give all of the praise to the One who saved me!

FLOATING IN AIR AND REMEMBERING

It was many years after we were married that my husband finally told me the whole story about his accident the winter before I met him. I had seen him driving around the block near the apartment where I lived with my mother and sister. He was the most handsome fellow I'd ever seen, and I had a mad crush on him, even though we had never met. One day he disappeared, and I thought my Prince Charming was a lost cause.

This is the story as he told it to me.

It was hard for me to grasp what was happening. I was high in the corner of a cold, impersonal ER. I could see a doctor doing something to my body. I felt completely alone. My mother was on her knees beside the gurney, praying; I'd never seen her pray before. Her prayers were a combination of pleas for my recovery as well as forgiveness for the sense of guilt she felt.

The white-haired doctor turned to her and said, "He's gone. There isn't anything I can do for him." Then he covered my face with a sheet.

I tried to talk to them, to holler to them, to say I was right there, but nobody could hear me. I lost all sense of time and space. All of my life, I'd felt I was being protected by something, but now, I felt completely alone.

Suddenly, I floated through the ceiling into gray, swirling clouds. I knew I was going backward in time. I saw myself in the Philippines in combat in World War II. I saw the time I nearly was shot by a Japanese soldier, and saved by an alert buddy; and then I saw the time their mortar fire had zeroed in on my foxhole and machine gun, and I escaped by the skin of my teeth.

Then I travelled through time again, and I saw myself as a twelve-year-old walking on a street in Detroit, Michigan. The police were chasing a hit-and-run driver, who proceeded to hit me too. He never stopped, but kept speeding away from the scene with the police in pursuit. Witnesses told my mother that my body flew over twenty feet in the air, and as I came down, I hit the door handle of the police car, which broke my nose and one leg.

The next thing I saw was when I was about five, living with my grandparents. I had fallen through a large window, severing an artery in my right leg. They rushed me to a doctor who sewed it up, but told them I had lost too much blood to survive. My grandmother refused to hear that, telling him she knew that I would be healed, and that was the end of the discussion.

I had lived all of this time and now I'm home after two years in the army during the war, and what have I done? Even though I felt alone, I could see that over the years I had been protected by something. It must be God—the One my grandmother kept telling me about. She told me that He had a plan for my life and I should listen to Him. He would lead me where He wanted me to go. Is this all a part of that plan? It seemed like a mighty strange plan, I thought as I tumbled over and over in the gray clouds through something like a tunnel.

I tried to remember what had happened and how I'd gotten to this point. We had a big snow, and I was surprised that my mother had driven out from Detroit in that weather. She insisted that I come home for lunch with her and my grandparents, even though she knew I had to work in the afternoon.

I remembered driving fast—too fast for the conditions. Then I remembered breaking over a small hill and seeing a car parked in the middle of the road and a child walking on the other side. There was no place for me to go. To avoid hitting one of them, I aimed the car for the school grounds, trying to go between two trees. Apparently, I hit a patch of ice and the car slid into the huge oak tree. The car jammed into the tree, driving the steering wheel into the back seat. I was partially thrown out of the car; one foot was pinned between the pedals. My skull was fractured, the right leg was shattered, and my left arm was broken.

I'd had close calls before, but never had I been able to look down and see what was happening. Suddenly, I was back in the corner of the ER again. My mother still knelt on her knees; the nurses tried to move her out of the way; they wanted to move the gurney and clean up the room.

I hovered there, watching, feeling very tired. Suddenly, I found myself back inside of my body. Someone who was tending me must have seen something move—a finger twitch or something. They ran to the door shouting, "He's alive! He moved!"

The doctor checked me again, and he grudgingly agreed to have me admitted to a hospital bed. He put my arm and leg in traction, saying he didn't want to waste his time setting the bones, as I wouldn't come out of it anyway. They told me later than I was in a coma for over two weeks.

I didn't have any sense of time or memory during that period. It wasn't until I felt an excruciating sense of pain that brought me back to reality, and I realized I was in bad shape.

Another doctor took me to the OR to set my broken bones, and then they kept me heavily sedated. Through the drug-induced haze, my mind kept remembering my grandmother's voice saying, "God has a plan for your life. Pay attention to Him."

As Howard's body healed, he spent much time thinking about those words. As the years rolled past, we both realized that God did have a plan for his life indeed.

We met after he was healed and able to return to work. His friend had been going with my sister, and the two guys arranged a blind date for me to meet him. I didn't know it then, but he had already told his friend that he'd been watching me while he was driving around. He said he knew then that I was the girl he was going to marry!

We had five children, thirteen grandchildren, and before he went home to be with the Lord, we also had twelve great-grandchildren.

There definitely was a plan for his life, and not only for his.

In Jeremiah 1:5, the Lord says, "Before I shaped you in your mother's womb, I knew all about you. Before you saw the light of day, I had holy plans for you. (THE MESSAGE)

He knows and loves each one of us. Each is important to Him.

ON BEING WEIGHTED DOWN

In my devotional books, I often read of people's reaction to the problems of life, the situations which can be so terribly depressing we feel as if we are carrying a heavy weight. We may literally bend over under the weight or in our mind feel as though we are stooped.

I remember one time when my husband and I were in northern Michigan during deer season. We had made our camp, and after lunch had gone back into the woods. We hadn't seen any deer all day, but we did enjoy walking through the trees, listening to the sounds of the birds and other creatures.

We had walked for a long time, and I suggested that it might be a good time to start back to the tent. He agreed, and we headed in the direction he chose. We walked and walked; it seemed that hours had passed by.

I asked him if he was sure we were going in the right direction, and he insisted we were, as he'd checked his compass before we left the camp. I couldn't argue with a compass, so I continued following him.

As the afternoon wore on, I grew more tired. The sun was very warm, and I was overheated in the heavy clothes I wore. The weight of the rifle I carried seemed to increase with each step we took until I was about ready to drop it and leave it behind. Of course, I couldn't actually do that.

Then we came across a logging trail. He started to cross it and I insisted we stop to rest a bit. I told him we hadn't crossed any trails before, and if we did this time, we'd probably end up in the deepest part of the forest.

We exchanged a few unkind words; he was tired too. Finally, I insisted that he check his compass again. Grudgingly, he put his rifle down beside a tree and took another look at it. The expression on his face told me what I was thinking had been right.

All this time he'd checked the compass while carrying the rifle, and the metal in it had thrown the needle off. We were going in the wrong direction! We did make it back to our camp in a matter of time, footsore, tired, and irritable, but back.

Many times in life we have similar experiences—times when we think we are going in the right direction, but we are off course. Some burdens we carry can pull our moral compass away from true north. That burden may be guilt for something we have done or for something we have left undone.

It is only when we cast down these burdens and we check our course again that we will make it home safely.

We must allow the Holy Spirit to be our true north, and then He will guide us safely through any situation in which we find ourselves.

The only safe way to travel is by asking the Holy Spirit to take the lead, and then submit to His perfect direction.

BURNING DAYLIGHT

It was in the winter of 1978 that we were able to take our first extended vacation. We'd had many long weekends and short getaways, but this was the first actual two-week vacation.

It was a bitter cold day as we packed our station wagon and headed south to Florida. In my mind's eye, I can still see our youngest daughter. She was bundled in a snowmobile suit, wrapped in a blanket, and trying to sleep off the cold she'd had for a few days. Our four older children were grown and busy with their own lives, so it was just the three of us in the car.

We made a stop in Kentucky for a short visit with our oldest daughter and her family, and then we headed to the Carolinas and on to "paradise."

By the end of the second day, we were able to peel off a few layers of clothes and turn down the car heater. We stopped at all the tourist traps along I-95 and the east coast, before we headed west from the Miami area to see what that coastline had to offer.

One night we stayed at a lovely place with a pool. Remember, this was early February, and we were tourists. We went down to the pool and wondered why everyone was just sitting around in the chairs. Dad was undaunted. He jumped into the pool and was having a good time all by himself, when a lady asked him if the water was too cold.

"No," He replied. "It feels good."

The poor soul believed him and she jumped in. As she surfaced, she came up screaming.

"You liar!" She gasped for air as she coughed and choked on the water she had swallowed.

Everyone around had a good laugh at her expense. Looking back now, I can see where it might possibly have caused her to have a heart attack or something due to how difficult it was for her to catch her breath.

It had been a marvelous time. The only complaint we females had was that Dad didn't want to stop for the night until it was dark.

"We're burning daylight!" he'd say.

We headed north through areas such as Naples, Pt. Charlotte, etc. About six thirty or so, we were tired and hungry and finally managed to coax Howard to stop to find a room.

Every motel had their *no vacancy* signs out. We kept driving north, looking for a room, but it wasn't until nearly midnight that we found a place. We checked in, and as we carried our bags to our room, we understood why they had a vacancy. If I say the housekeeping left much to be desired, that should tell you what the room was like.

If it had not been so late and we were not so tired, we'd have gotten in the car and left. But it was, and we were, so we didn't.

We didn't peel back the bedding, but just lay on top of it in our clothes. We tried desperately not to think about what sort of little critters might be moving around in the dark.

As daylight crept in, we had no trouble waking up. When we went out to the car, we could see just how tacky and undesirable the place was. At one time, it may have been a cozy place for the military people at the nearby base. Now, it looked as if it there the original "No Tell Motel."

After that experience, we were able to convince Dad it was better to stop earlier in the day —about three to four o'clock p.m.—have a nice dinner someplace, and get some rest by going to bed early. That way the time on the road he thought we would lose, we could actually make up by getting the early start.

Burning daylight was no longer a problem.

1 Corinthians 9:17 says, "I have been entrusted with a stewardship." (NKJV) These words don't just mean we should be wise in handling money; it also includes good management of time.

God expects us to use good sense in everything, especially where our or someone else's health may be concerned.

WHAT IS BETTER THAN TWO?

In the early 1980's we sold our house in town to move to one in the country. We were both thrilled at the prospect of being back in a rural setting, although we knew there was much to be done to the house.

Our first priority had to be to build a garage. The house needed a lot of work, but the garage was a "must have." It had to be used for storage until the work in the house was completed.

My husband and a friend laid out and poured the footings for the thirty-six foot square building, and poured the concrete floor. Surrounded by grass and abutting the house, the slab looked terribly large.

My carpenter husband had all of the materials required to frame the building delivered, and working by himself, he began to build the walls.

It was on a Saturday morning I learned about the power of a man and a lever. Howard was most anxious to get the walls standing so he could tie them together.

As we ate breakfast that morning, he calmly said, "When we're done, let's go out and raise the east wall first. There aren't any windows in it, so it is the heaviest."

My mouth fell open as I tried to grasp the concept that he honestly believed that he and I alone could handle that monstrous assemblage of lumber. I had learned over the years that when he put his mind to do something, it would be done, so I didn't totally freak out and run away screaming.

With a strange feeling in the pit of my stomach, I watched as he took three, long two-by-fours and nailed them loosely into both ends and the center of the structure.

"Now," he said, "you take the end of that one, and I'll take this one. We'll just slowly walk them up, and as we do, they will lift the wall before them.

"What about the third piece?" I asked, less than enthused.

"Don't worry about that now," he said. "Just go slow and steady, and we'll be fine."

As we raised the wall, it resisted our efforts. I soon became tired.

"Just kick the brace against the floor and keep your foot on it," Howard told me. He did the same thing, and it amazed me to see that monster wall stand there on an angle. He went to the brace in the center section, lifted it to match the first two, and jammed it toward the floor.

Mentally, I agonized over what might have happened next. My imagination worked overtime, visualizing all sorts of wild, tragic events occurring.

"Ready?" he asked as he prepared to complete the move.

About that time we heard the sounds of tires crunching on the gravel driveway. It was our daughter-in-law stopping in to say hello. Before she knew what happened, she had been assigned to the third brace.

With the three of us working together, the structure was standing within a few minutes. We repeated the process of bracing the wall against the floor while my husband went to get his long level and tool belt. It took only a few minutes for him to nail one end firmly to the side of the house.

We females were quite impressed at what we had been able to do, but before we had time to brag, he was ready to raise the opposite wall. The entire process was repeated, and we were proud to see two, thirty-six-foot-long walls of studs, standing straight upright. The next step was to raise the south wall, which had openings for two, large doors.

I thought that would be a cinch compared to the first two. I hadn't even considered how heavy it would be with the huge beams he'd built to support the openings for two doors. That job went well too, and soon he excused us from duty while he made certain that all sides were plumb and properly tied together, ready to stand up to any weather.

We ladies went inside to have coffee, relax, and marvel at what we had done. It truly was scriptural. Parts of Ecclesiastes read, "Two are better than one. . . if they fall, one will lift up his companion. . . but a threefold cord is not quickly broken." (NKJV)

EXPLORING SPIRITUAL THINGS

It was in the late 1960's and early 1970's when I began to explore spiritual things. I had always been involved in church, and it was during that time we were exposed to pastors of what was called "the new school." That meant that they didn't really accept all of the teachings of the Bible. We knew enough about the Lord to know they were wrong, but not enough to really search for Him in the right way.

I became involved with a group of people who intended to help me develop my spiritual gifts: ESP, automatic writing, etc. These people wore the cloak of Christianity, but they taught something totally different from what the apostles instructed the Church.

I knew in my heart I was getting into something over my head, which could be dangerous, but I kept plodding along with their teachings.

Looking back now, I can see where the Holy Spirit protected me and tried to keep me from error. One night I had a very graphic dream. In that dream, I was driving my car, and somehow the front wheels veered to the right side of the road, high on a step bank overlooking the sea. The more I tried to right the wheels and turn away, the further the car slipped. Finally, in the dream I jumped out of the vehicle and scrambled back up the hill and watched the car go into the water.

It took many months and a few years of wandering and searching for the truth until I committed my life to the Lord. Watching the TV evangelists was wonderful, but I knew I had to find a church which would build me spiritually and edify me.

Doing word studies on *pastors* and *shepherds*, I searched the Scriptures for the truth. These are a few of the verses which God took me to.

> "My sheep wandered through all the mountains, and on every high hill, yes, My flock was scattered over the whole face of the earth and no one was seeking or searching for them."
> (Ezekiel 34:6 NKJV)

> "And I will give you shepherds according to My heart, who will feed you with the knowledge and understanding." (Jeremiah 3:15 NKJV)

> "My sheep hear My voice, and I know them, and they follow Me."
> (John 10:27 NKJV)

I prayed and asked God to lead me to a church where I could be taught and grow in His Word and wisdom. He did just that!

While running errands regularly, I had passed a small church and never noticed it. Suddenly, every time I went by, I'd turn my head to look at it. On the return trip, I felt compelled to look at it again. I was drawn to it without knowing anything about it.

Finally, I got the point; the next time I passed the church and a car was there, I stopped in. I met a lovely lady who greeted me as a long lost sister and invited me to join them next Sunday morning. I did and that became my home church. The pastor was exactly the type of teacher I had been looking for.

God made me another Promise.

> "Behold, the tabernacle of God is with men, and He will dwell with them, and they shall be His people. God Himself will be with them and be their God." (Revelation 21:3 NKJV)

I asked Him about those false teachers and what would happen to them, and He told me the following.

> "'Woe to the shepherds who destroy and scatter the sheep of My pasture!' says the LORD. . . 'You have scattered My flock, driven them away, and not attended to them. Behold, I will attend to you for the evil of your doings. . . I will gather the remnant of My flock out of all countries. . . I will set up shepherds over them who will feed them; and they shall fear no more, nor be dismayed, nor shall they be lacking,' says the LORD." (Jeremiah 23:1-4 NKJV)

How can I thank Him for loving me, protecting me, and leading me in the paths He would have me follow? All I can do is praise the Lord—this Lord who personally went looking for me!

KIT AND MABEL

When I met the young man whom I would marry, he took me to meet his grandparents. They were the ones who had the most to do with raising him, and they were the first people in his family was introduced to.

I knew the moment I met them that I was home where I belonged. I often would tease him and say the only reason I married him was to get his grandparents. I never had a chance to know my own. My mother's mother died long before I was born, and my dad's parents died when I was quite young.

When these two people took me in like a mother hen does her chicks, I was ready, willing, and anxious to call them my own.

They lived on a small farm without a tractor. The heavy work was done with the aid of two strong horses named Kit and Mabel. I didn't learn until years later that they were named after the wives of the adjacent farmers. I'm sure there was a story behind that, but I never heard it. I wonder what I missed.

On one occasion, the two of us wanted to surprise Granddad by having the horses hitched and ready for him to go to work. When he came into the barn, he was quick to tell us that he really did appreciate our efforts, but we had done it all wrong.

As he quickly unhitched them and moved them around, he said that Mabel *had to be* on the right side of Kit. We couldn't see what possible difference that could make, but we listened as he went on.

Without even looking at what he was doing, he told us that Mabel had a tendency to drift from side to side. If she were on the left, she would pull strongly in whatever direction she would choose that given day. Kit, being of a more agreeable sort, would just follow her lead without arguing about it.

That would make the job more difficult for him. While walking behind them as they pulled the plow, or whichever tool was being used, he would have a mighty struggle trying to keep his furrows in a straight line.

When Kit was on the left, she was a strong leader. She would pull in a straight line, and Mabel was content to follower her without any struggle for power.

I've since learned that our human nature is such that we often tend to go off in all directions—usually the wrong ones. We can wander off on some tangent until we find ourselves lost or in trouble.

However, if we attach our lines to the One who is a strong leader, He will keep us going in the straight path.

"My soul follows close beside You." (Psalm 63:18 NKJV)

Let us strive to keep that as our motto in our life.

MY FIRST PERMANENT

When I was quite young—I can't remember how old I was—my mother thought I might look good with curly hair. To appreciate the thought of me with curls, it is important to know that my hair is by nature straight—very straight.

All of this happened long before the days of the *Toni Home Permanent*. That product didn't come on the market until the post-war days of the 1940's and early 1950's.

Mother made an appointment with the lady who did her hair so I could be given a *permanent wave*. I had no idea what to expect when I entered Pearl Pipp's Beauty Salon. That was her real name. Who could make up a name like hat?

I was sure I could learn to appreciate the shampoo part of the procedure. Lying back in a chair with my head over a sink and the lady gently scrubbing my hair felt like a bit of heaven.

When Mother did it at home, I had to stand on a stool and hold my head under the faucet. She made me hold a rolled-up towel to my eyes so the soapy water wouldn't get in them. Then came the hardest part of the project; Mother insisted that I stand still.

"Stop wiggling, and I don't want to hear the water is too hot or too cold."

The only thing I hated worse than the shampoo was when she combed my hair. She always had my hair cut into a *Dutch Boy Bob*. That meant perfectly straight with bangs on my forehead and cut short enough all around so that only the tips of my earlobes would show.

I never could figure out how I could get so many snarls in hair that short, but I did. Mother never used a brush—always just a comb. When she hit a snarl, she just pulled harder until the pesky thing was gone.

It hurt! Of course, I cried, and that only upset her more, which made me want to move more, which made her pull harder. Not a good memory.

But, I digress.

I enjoyed the shampooing process at Pearl Pipp's Beauty Salon and felt very grown-up. When she finished washing my hair, I followed Pearl toward a device which looked as if it could have been used as a torture machine. I could see it operated on electricity. It had a big cable running from its base to the largest electrical outlet I'd ever seen. The cable hung down from a huge, round, dome-shaped thing with dozens of big wires attached to it. Suspended from these wires were huge clamps. The whole thing was located directly above a chair, which appeared to be waiting for its next victim. I had no idea what would come next, but just by looking at it made shivers of fear run down my spine.

I was relieved when Pearl directed me to a different chair. That was where she parted and sectioned off my entire scalp, then put on some big curlers.

About the time I began to relax again, she told me to follow her to that fearsome device. I was ready to run for the door, but Mother was in front of it. I didn't know much about that machine, but I did know my mother well enough not to mess with her when she had that look on her face.

I meekly followed Pearl, sat in that chair, and began to pray as she attached the cables to the curlers in my hair. She tried to explain to me about the chemical reaction of the stuff she had put on my hair and the heat which came from the electrical circuits. I didn't even pretend to listen to her. I was too busy praying, asking St. Jude, the patron saint of lost causes, to help me.

I don't remember how long I had to sit there, tied to that machine. All I can remember is wondering what would happen to me if the building caught on fire. I could see the newspaper. *Poor little Patty O'Brien burned to death chained to a machine.*

I ended up with a head full of curls, but I certainly didn't remind anyone of Shirley Temple. I don't remember how long the curls lasted. The wave was not permanent as I had been led to believe, and it wasn't too long before the Dutch Boy Bob came back.

I made a decision that day to never again allow anyone to hook me up to a device like that.

I've made other decisions in my life, but the most important one was made in the spring of 1976. That was when I surrendered myself— body, soul and spirit—to the Lord. I decided to commit myself to serving God in gratitude for the sacrifice His Son made for me.

Galatians 2:20 says it best for me. "I lived by faith in the Son of God. Who loved me, and gave Himself for me." (NKJV)

That decision was made over thirty years ago, and I have never regretted it since. Have you made that decision for yourself?

DANCING WITH DANNY

The first year of our marriage, we lived much the same as other couples our age. My husband and most of the men in our circle of friends were veterans, returning from World War II. Those fellows who hadn't seen combat had been stationed in Germany, Japan, and other countries.

We wives were quite young; some had a bit of college, but most of us had taken jobs as we left school.

As the boys came home, some of them took advantage of the GI Bill of Rights. That was a government program designed to help returning vets finance a college education.

Others went the route of the "52/20 Club". This program gave them twenty dollars a week for fifty-two weeks. It was supposed to give the fellows time to readjust to civilian life. Unfortunately, the greatest share of them used it as an excuse to do nothing but drink and have a good time.

There was another group. When they got home, all they wanted to do was get a decent job, marry, and make a better life for themselves than their folks had had.

My husband fell into that last group. He went back to the auto mechanic work he'd been doing before he went in to the army. His employer sent him to the Oldsmobile Factory School in Lansing, Michigan, where he learned all there was to know about the making, repairing, assembling and disassembling of their automatic transmission known as the *Hydramatic*.

In addition to having military experience in common, they all loved cars, talking about them, working on them, and even racing them. Since few of them could afford the new post-war models, most of them had vehicles dating back to the late 1930's. The favorite model was the 1940 Ford—any model.

Our small town didn't have much to offer in the line of night life. There were a couple of bars in town, but the young fellows didn't go there, as they pretty much catered to the older crowd. Returning vets were generally considered to be "trouble waiting to happen."

Just west of town on the crest of a high hill was a place with the unique name of "Hilltop Bar". In addition to the libations they provided at the bar, they also served food, burgers, fries, etc. On Friday and Saturday evenings, often there would be a small combo, who played the music of the era—great to listen to, greater still to dance to.

Some of the folks could cut a mean rug; for you young folks, that means they were jitterbugs and swing dancers. Others would enjoy the slower music of the two-step with their favorite girl. All in all, Hilltop was a good place to go on a Friday evening.

On one of those evenings, we were there with another couple, who happened to be dancing. My husband and I were left alone at the table when something happened.

A young man I knew named Danny came over and asked my husband's permission to ask me to dance with him. My guy had never met him, even though they had run into each other once or twice before. He worked at the same place as my mother, and I had met him there.

"I don't care. If she wants to, "Howard mumbled.

Danny extended his hand to me and said, "Shall we?" We had one dance before the band picked up the beat, and I told him I'd had enough.

When I got back to the table, my husband was doing his impression of the great stone face. When we started home, I asked him, "Why are you acting like this? You said you didn't care if I danced with him. Why be so nasty now?"

A very long silence.

"I said I didn't care, if you wanted to," he sulked.

"So why are you acting so angry?"

After another long silence,

"Because, I didn't think you'd want to," he growled.

The next few hours passed in a cold truce, but what he'd said stuck in my mind. *He didn't think I'd want to.*

Thank God I had enough sense to realize what he was saying behind the words he used. This other guy was over six-feet tall, really nice looking—even handsome. My guy was not ugly, but handsome is not a word which would apply to him. Cute, yes, handsome, no.

I realized that when I wanted to dance with someone other than him, he felt as if I were putting him down or rejecting him. I took that lesson to heart and put in the file labeled, *I'll never do that again.*

After more than sixty years later, that event was brought to my remembrance because I needed to have something to illustrate a point in a Bible study I'd prepared. We were in the book of Hosea, chapter 8. The Israelites had become so involved with those who worshipped idols that they easily fell into joining them in their worship.

I had recalled the times my mother would say, "If you lay down with a dog, don't be surprised if you get fleas," and the old faithful, "If you play with fire you're going to get burned."

During the class, I struggled to make the point, when with no warning, the story of my dance with Danny, a tale long since forgotten, tumbled out of my mouth. Thanking back, I realized how easily I could have fallen into a situation where I could have sinned, not just in my imagination, but in reality. I could have risked my marriage and everything precious to me.

That was not the first time I found words coming out of my mouth through the power of the Holy Spirit, but it certainly was the most dramatic in my eyes.

I'm not the first person to have that experience. The Old Testament is full of stories of that happening. It happened to Moses in Exodus 4:12, to Balaam in Numbers 23:5, and to Isaiah in 51:16, to Jeremiah in 1:9. They were all given the same promise. "I will put words in your mouth."

That promise is not just to the Old Testament saints, but also for us today.

There may come a day when our very life or death may depend on how faithful we are and what words we will use to honor the Lord. Whether it is a situation like that or, in a group of a few people, and you try to share with others your love for the Lord whenever you really need to express your relationship with the Lord. He will give you the words if you truly believe Him.

"Make up your mind right now, not to worry about it. I will give you words and wisdom." (Luke 21:14-15 THE MESSAGE)

That promise is repeated in Mark 3, and also in Luke 12.

But my favorite is in 1 Thessalonians 5:24. "The One Who called you is completely dependable. If He said it, He will do it. (THE MESSAGE)

VAPOR TRAILS

Early one spring morning, just before the sun came up, I took my little dog outside so she could tend to her morning chores. It was the kind of morning the Florida Chamber of Commerce boasts about; the sky was beautiful blue with not a cloud in sight, and the temperature was warm enough that even in my pajamas, I was comfortable. There was little or no breeze and the air smelled fresh and clean.

While I waited for her to finish, I looked at the sky. I saw a vapor trail high above me running from the northeast to the southwest. Of course, it traced the route of a very large jet plane. The air, even at that altitude, was still, so the trail lasted until the plane disappeared beyond the horizon.

My imagination took over as I wondered where the people aboard had come from and where they were going. Who were the people? Was it a military aircraft with a crew on a training mission or ferrying equipment from one base to another? Was it a cargo plane carrying packages from folks to their loved ones or delivering parcels for a freight company? Was it a passenger plane loaded with people travelling from the northeastern states to somewhere west or perhaps to Texas?

Whatever the truth of that flight, I was sure of one thing; the plane was real, and it had left a trail behind it that showed its course.

Should my life be like that airplane? As I live my life, telling the world that I am claiming Jesus as my Savior and Lord of my life, do I leave a vapor trail?

Can people look at the way I behave and tell the direction I am heading as well as sense my destination? Can they look at my life and see something which makes me appear to be different than the rest of the world?

I pray the Lord will help me to be the light Jesus spoke of in Mathew 5:14, 16. "A city that is set on a hill, cannot be hidden. . . Let your light so shine before men, that they may see your good works and glorify your Father in heaven." (THE MESSAGE)

THE LAST LOVE LETTER

My husband was not the kind of man who could not express his emotions verbally. His grandparents who had raised him were of the old school and felt that expressing one's emotions was a sign of weakness.

I had been raised in an openly affectionate family. Hugs and love-pats, as well as terms of endearment were a part of ordinary, daily life.

It should have been apparent to all the two backgrounds would collide. It didn't take long. When the starvation for affection set in, I began to feel I was a burden he had to carry. One day, while in tears, I asked Howard if he still loved me.

"I married you, didn't I? If anything changes, I'll let you know."

Somehow God was able to make me understand why he couldn't say it. He enabled me to see that he was showing me every day in many ways that he really did love me. I cannot take the credit for the maturity it took for me to fully grasp the concept. It was only the wisdom God had given me.

I remember one Valentine's Day while we ate breakfast I asked him if he would get me a valentine. He took the ever-present red pencil from his shirt pocket and drew a heart with an arrow through it.

"Now you can't say I never gave you a valentine," he said as he slid it across the table to me.

I kept it in a frame for a long time, as it was a special treasure to me.

As the years passed, I learned to be content with the fact that he was different than me, and that I must accept him as he was. The years went by—fifty-seven of them.

Valentine's Day rolled around in 2004. Howard's health had been failing and he was very weak. That day he felt well enough to go for a drive and stop at his favorite place to get smoked fish. After we picked up his goodies, we drove aimlessly, enjoying the beauty of our area of Florida.

As I drove, he suddenly reached over and took my hand. He commented that today was Valentine's Day. After a pause, he said, "I don't have to worry about that. I already have my valentine, don't I?"

Tears instantly filled my eyes as I tried to pay attention to the road.

He passed away on February 27th, 2004. When I began the task of sorting out his things, I ran across the little spiral-bound booklet in which he kept a record of his blood sugar readings. The pages were nearly filled, and I casually tossed it toward the wastebasket. It fell open to a page which I had missed while flipping through it only moments before.

On that page he had printed my name eleven times. He had used three different colored pens and different styles of printing. On the bottom of the page, in bright red letters were the words, *I love Patricia*.

Obviously, nothing had changed.

KEEP HOLD OF GOD'S HAND

In the winter of 1988 the devil and his legions attacked our family, wounding us in such an unbelievable manner. As a result of that attack, we found ourselves in a courtroom facing a judge, who made no secret of his intentions to try to destroy our family. He ordered two of our grandchildren to be taken from their father and his parental rights terminated.

The judge looked us square in our eyes. "As far as you are concerned," he said, "these children were never born. You will never see them again."

The last time I was to see them, the boy was eight and his little sister not quite seven. Thanks to a kind-hearted worker for the state, she arranged for us to see them before they were taken and moved several hundred miles away.

I spoke to the little guy and told him the story of how when Moses was a baby, his mother had to send him away to keep her boy safe from harm and that she trusted God to bring him to someone would care for him and truly love him.

I told him that this day I was doing the same thing. He and his sister would be going away from our family, but that I was praying that God would keep the two of them safe. I asked God to send them to someone who would love them and care for them.

Just as Moses did return to his parent's home in his adult years, I prayed that God would also bring these two children back to our family. I entrusted them to God's eternal care and protection. I had to. I had no other choice.

With my heart breaking, I hugged them and kissed them both. Then I had to turn and walk away from them with no way of knowing if I would ever see them again in this world.

The years went by, and often someone would ask if we'd heard anything from the children. I would have to answer, "No, not yet." In my heart, I clung to the promises God made to those who love Him. I knew that someday He would bring them back to our family.

It was a bit over eleven years later, when one day the phone rang. A young, male voice asked if my son was there.

"No, he isn't," I replied. "But can I take a message for him?" The caller stated that he would try again another time.

Before I hung up the phone, I knew it was my grandson! Telling my husband about the call, I wept for joy. Then I realized I didn't have any information about how to call him back.

We thanked God when the phone rang again. I answered the phone.

"Are you my grandma?" the young, male voice asked.

We had a great conversation on the phone, and I discovered he was about one hundred fifty miles north of our home. He gave us directions how to find him. A little more than two hours later, we drove down the long lane, and a tall, gangly, young man stepped out of the door and approached me.

I grabbed him, held him in my arms, and all I could say was, "Thank You, Jesus! Thank You, Jesus!" over and over again.

I could have picked him out of twenty or more boys. He looked exactly the same, just a bit taller. We haven't yet been blessed by having his sister restored to us, but I know in time she too will come. He keeps in touch with her, and when she's ready, he'll bring her to us.

> "Call to me and I will answer you and show you great and mighty things which you do not know." (Jeremiah 33:3 NKJV)
> "I am the LORD, thy God of all flesh. Is anything too hard for Me?" (Jeremiah 32:27 NKJV)
> "Fear not for I am with you: be not dismayed, for I am your God. I will strengthen you, yes, I will help you, I will uphold you with My righteous right hand." (Isaiah 41:10 NKJV)

I have learned to hold fast to God's unchanging hand. He has never let me down.

Praise the Lord!

PSALM 17:15

We humans are indeed strange creatures. We think we are very intelligent and well informed. When it comes to being aware of what is happening in our own body, we often kid ourselves. We ignore warning signals, which are trying to alert us to the fact that our "machine" is in trouble.

I recently had one such episode. My mind and will were wrapped up in my plans to fly to my previous home in Michigan, the people I would see, and the places I wanted to visit. All I could think of was what I wanted to do and chose to pay no attention to the shortness of breath I had been experiencing. Then one day it suddenly became something I could no longer ignore.

When I called my daughter, she immediately took me to the local Emergency Room. Normally, there are great piles of paperwork involved in that little matter; however, this visit I was whisked away to be cared for so quickly I was barely aware of what was happening. Looking back now, I have trouble remembering exactly what did happen.

The memories are blurred. Several doctors and medical technicians were engrossed in the information they received from the different electronic machines attached to my body. My daughter and her husband were standing nearby watching the activity, looking very concerned. I heard a nurse tell them that "your mother is one, very sick lady."

Then someone told me they were going to put me in an ambulance and take me to the larger hospital nearby. It had a new Cardiac Care Unit where I could be treated. I recognized the bumpy road which led to the main route because I had driven it myself so many times. My pastor popped in for a few seconds to have prayer with me. I remember the cardiac surgeon spoke with me and had prayer with me.

Then a very large man, the anesthesiologist, told me to think of something pleasant.

"When you wake up," he said, "you'll feel much better."

Those are the few things which stuck in my mind most.

Think of something pleasant.

In the days prior to this event I had been preparing a Bible study in Psalms 17: 15. It came to my mind now. "As for me, I will behold Thy face in righteousness; I shall be satisfied, when I awake with Thy likeness." (KJV)

THE MESSAGE puts that text this way. "As for me, I plan on looking You full in the face. When I get up, I'll see Your full stature and live heaven on earth!"

Who could imagine anything more pleasant to think about?

They told me later that the pericardia, a sac which is around the heart, had filled with fluids.

I knew my feet and legs had been swollen, and I also knew that meant my body was retaining fluids. I had no idea of how serious my condition was.

They explained to me later that the cardiac surgeon had "put a window" in that sac. This allowed the fluids to drain through a tube in my side, and prevented it from building up again.

If you have read this book so far, you should be very aware of the fact that I live with a deep and abiding faith in the Lord Jesus Christ. That faith has been my strength in the good times, as well as in those not so good times. I know deep in my heart that God has a plan for my life.

I made that decision many years ago, and I thank God that I did. You see, if I hadn't done it, I would never have gone in to that operating room with that calm assurance that, "As for me, I plan on looking You full in the face. When I get up, I'll see Your full stature and live heaven on earth."

In this country the gospel has been preached effectively for so many years, that surely everybody had heard the message at least one time. I wonder how many humans in the back of our minds believe that we will always have time to "made a decision for Christ." We procrastinate and want to put off until tomorrow what we could do today. But, who is promised tomorrow?

You see, I had no idea that death was as near as it really was. My mind had sold me the idea that I just had a little problem. I was intent on making the trip I had planned. Now I understand that the only reason I am still alive is that God has something more He wants me to do. When and only when, I have completed His assignment, He will call me home to be with Him in heaven.

His love for the human race is so great it is beyond what our simple minds can comprehend. He made us because He wanted to have companionship, to have somebody to love who would love Him in return.

He also made us to have a free will, to have the opportunity to choose to love Him or not. I have chosen to love Him and to devote my life to serving

Him in ways which will bring honor to Him. I want to serve Him in this life and to spend eternity with Him and all of His saints in the glory of heaven.

I cannot grasp why there are some people who would choose not to love Him, not want to serve Him, or to spend eternity with Him, when they have the opportunity to do so.

It is so simple. He sent His son Jesus to earth because He loved His creation.

In THE MESSAGE, John 3:16 states it so clearly.

> "This is how much God loved the world: He gave his Son, his one and only Son. And this is why: so that no one need be destroyed; by believing in him, anyone can have a whole and lasting life. God didn't go to all the trouble of sending his Son merely to point an accusing finger, telling the world how bad it was. He came to help, to put the world right again. Anyone who trusts in him is acquitted; anyone who refuses to trust him has long since been under the death sentence without knowing it. And why? **Because of that person's failure to believe in the one-of-a-kind Son of God when introduced to him.**" (Bold is by the author for effect.)

All we have to do is believe that promise and claim it for ourselves. It doesn't matter if we grew up in a church, or if our parents are sincere believers; it is a choice we must make for ourselves.

The last part of Galatians 2:20 makes it very personal.

> "I live by the faith of the Son of God, who loved ME, and gave Himself for ME." (Capitalization of the word *me* is by the author for effect.)

Romans 1:17 tells us,

> "The just shall live by faith." We don't need to do anything crazy or outlandish; just simply claim that promise for our life—now and for eternity.

In THE MESSAGE, Romans 12:1 tells us,

> "So here's what I want you to do, God helping you: Take your everyday, ordinary life—your sleeping, eating, going-to-work, and walking-around life—and place it before God as an offering. Embracing what God does for you is the best thing you can do for him."

If you have never made that choice, you can do it right now while you're sitting there reading this book. All you have to do is say this prayer:

"God, I thank You for sending Your Son Jesus to save those who will choose to believe. I do believe that Jesus died for me, and I ask You to forgive my sins in His name. Lord, I want to spend the rest of my life serving You. Please send Jesus to live in my heart and to help me to be the person You want me to be When it comes to my time to meet death, please give me the peace this writer spoke of, to know that when I "get up" I will see Your face and be with You." Amen.

Now, wasn't that easy? One more thing you should do—go tell somebody what you just did, that you have asked Jesus to be Your Savior and to come live in your heart.

May God bless you as you begin your new life. I will keep you in my prayers.

LaVergne, TN USA
29 December 2009
168386LV00001B/1/P